BUSES OF SKYE
– AND THE –
WESTERN ISLES

JOHN SINCLAIR

AMBERLEY

By the time of the formation of the Scottish Transport Group in 1969, MacBrayne operated bus services on six islands, but within three years Highland Omnibuses had taken over on four of them, and the operations on North and South Uist had passed to private operators. Surprisingly, it was not until 1964 that MacBrayne obtained a presence on Harris, when the vehicles and premises of Tom Cameron, who owned the Harris Hotel Garage in Tarbert, were purchased. Of the two buses, only the eleven-seat Kenex-bodied Ford NST683 was operated. An attempt the previous year to buy the operation of John Mitchell of Stornoway, who also operated down to Harris, was not successful.

Dedicated to the memory of my friend Robert Grieves who shared my interest in the buses of the Highlands and Islands, and the companies that operated them.

First published 2014

Amberley Publishing
The Hill, Stroud
Gloucestershire, GL5 4EP

www.amberley-books.com

Copyright © John Sinclair, 2014

The right of John Sinclair to be identified as the Author of this work has been asserted in accordance with the Copyrights, Designs and Patents Act 1988.

ISBN 978 1 4456 2283 5 (paperback)
ISBN 978 1 4456 2297 2 (ebook)

British Library Cataloguing in Publication Data.
A catalogue record for this book is available from the British Library.

Typesetting by Amberley Publishing.
Printed in the UK.

Introduction

'The earth belongs unto the Lord and all that it contains, except the Western Islands and they are all MacBraynes.'

This well-known Highland quotation however concealed the truth that not all bus services on the islands were operated by MacBraynes, and this sequel to *Highland Buses* takes a look at the buses to be seen on Skye and the Western Isles during the 1960s and 1970s. The company continued with a policy of acquiring island operators right up until April 1970. By now, the MacBrayne empire encompassed bus services on North Uist, South Uist, Harris, Mull, Islay and Skye, as well as on the mainland. However, the Scottish Transport Group, formed in 1969, had decided that economies could be achieved by integrating the MacBrayne services with those of other STG companies, and in that very same month the vehicles and services of the Inverness area were taken over by Highland Omnibuses.

Over the next twenty-one months, the remainder of the MacBrayne fleet of 140 vehicles passed to Highland Omnibuses, with the exception of four Bedfords which went to Western SMT, four which went to private operators on Uist, and eighteen coaches which went to Alexander (Midland). Highland had already started to dispose of former MacBrayne routes that it considered to be financially unattractive when the Ardgour operation passed to Allan MacDonald of Acharacle in April 1971. This process continued until April 1976, when the vehicles and services on Mull were taken over by Bowman of Craignure, leaving Skye as the only remaining island on which Highland Omnibuses continued to have a presence. MacBraynes had never operated bus services on Lewis, although they had attempted to purchase the operation of John Mitchell of Stornoway in 1963, preparatory to the arrival of the car ferries being introduced the following year to open up the islands to tourism. It is interesting to speculate about whether there would today be a 'Stagecoach in the Western Isles' if that had been successful.

Much of this transformation I was able to witness first-hand. When I moved from Inverness to Stornoway in 1967 to continue with my surgical training, for the first time I found myself living on an island, where bus transport was almost exclusively in the hands of local operators. By good fortune, my friend Robert Grieves was driving MacBrayne coaches on extended tours, spending every second weekend on the island, and in this book I have included a few of his photographs in addition to my own.

As before, some of mine are of poor quality, being obtained from scans of prints where the original slides had not been returned by the dealer to whom I had lent them in the 1980s, particularly those on page 35. However, this book is intended to give a flavour of the variety of buses to be seen on the islands during this period of change, and the diverse terrain on which they operated.

The two major operators in Lewis in the 1960s had fleets of similar modern forty-two-seat Duple Midland-bodied Bedford SBs. Hebridean Transport, which operated all the services in the Eye Peninsula, had a fleet of nine, of which the oldest was only nine years old, and a solitary remaining Albion with a Duple coach body. Having bought six second-hand vehicles from Hutchison of Overtown between 1958 and 1960, HJS65 was the first of many new purchases, and is seen here approaching Portnaguran on a church run, before returning to Upper Bayble where it is outstationed.

John Mitchell of Stornoway operated the local services, and also those to other parts of the island, including Ness and the north-west. The north-east villages were his exclusive province, and EJS800E was only a year old when photographed in Glen Tolsta on the 6.00 service from Stornoway to Tolsta. It being a Friday night, it returned to Stornoway for the 10.45 p.m. run, being kept at High Tolsta overnight. One of twelve similar Bedfords with forty-two-seat Duple Midland bodies, all of which were operated from new, it was withdrawn in 1980 and ended up as a store at Lower Bayble.

Lochs Motor Transport of Crossbost had a small mixed fleet, which operated the 10-mile service from Stornoway to Ranish via Leurbost, in addition to school runs. On a mild February afternoon in 1968, waiting to collect children from Leurbost primary school are Bedford SB3 SK6348, bound for Cameron Terrace, and a 1963 eleven-seat Bedford VST554 for Balallan. Still in the livery of its previous owner, Steele of Carbost in Skye, it was sold to William MacDonald of Vatisker a year later. Kept at Balallan overnight, it also operated some of the service runs on Wednesday and Saturday.

The first bus on Lewis with power steering was a unique Dodge S306 model with a vertical Perkins engine in the front, and a forty-two-seat Weymann body. This was purchased from the manufacturer in January 1966 by Alexander MacDonald of Balallan. It had originally appeared as a demonstrator at a transport exhibition at Earl's Court in October 1962, entering service the following year. It was the first model made available by the company for British operators, remaining on sale for eight years, although few were sold. It was photographed carrying children on a private hire near Gress.

John Morrison, who lived in the village of Northton in South Harris, operated the through service from Tarbert to Stornoway, connecting Harris and Lewis, and also the services from Tarbert south to Rodel. This was effectively a circular route via the main road, travelling along the west coast by the beautiful sands of Luskentyre and the single-track road on the east side; it was known as the 'Golden Road' because it cost so much to build in 1897. This was even more spectacular, with rocky low-level scenery, and Bedford HCA177 is leaving Geocrab on the 2.30 p.m. service from Tarbert to Rodel.

Morrison's JVD623 is at Grosebay on a church run to Tarbert in August 1967, and was also a Motor Show exhibit at Kelvin Hall in Glasgow in 1953, in the livery of Northern Roadways. New to Hutchison of Overtown as a thirty-six-seat Duple Super Vega-bodied Bedford SBO with a diesel engine, it arrived in Northton in August 1964 from Fred Newton of Dingwall, after being operated by a number of companies – including Northern Roadways, who in fact bought it from Hutchison in May 1957. It was withdrawn before Highland Omnibuses took over Morrison's operation in June 1970.

In addition to the Friday-only service from Tarbert to the remote Harris community of Maruig, MacBrayne also acquired the school service, and WGG630 is approaching the terminus in April 1968. New in June 1959, it had operated from Ardvasar on Skye until January 1968, when it was transferred to Tarbert to replace the Ford, remaining as a school bus, but also used on tours and private hires, until the MacBrayne operation on Harris passed to Highland Omnibuses in June 1971. Not operated by them, it may have been allocated fleet number C23, although numbers C24 and C25 were never used.

Leaving Maruig, WGG630 is ascending to the main A859 road, before continuing north to Ardvourlie, where it turns round and returns to Tarbert. Classified as a Bedford C5Z, it had a forward-control truck chassis modified for PSV use, and such a rugged vehicle proved ideal for a rather basic road such as this. In addition, the ground clearance was particularly useful on the slips at the ferry terminals, and also when negotiating roads with grass in the middle, such as the stretch between Salen and Kilchoan. The twenty-nine-seater Duple coach was one of twenty-two similar vehicles new between 1958 and 1961.

Top: The other school run operated by MacBrayne, from Tarbert Academy, was east along the north shore of Loch Tarbert; it transferred the pupils to the tiny turntable ship for the five-minute crossing to Kyles of Scalpay. It was not until December 1997 that a bridge was finally opened to permit through traffic. Re-bodied Bedford FFS871, acquired with the operation of Cowe of Tobermory in May 1964, had moved to Harris in September 1966, and, while usually employed on tour work, occasionally covered the school services, and also the Scalpay mail run if there was no lorry available.

Middle: Another Bedford re-bodied with a Burlingham 'baby' Seagull body in 1953 was AST951, a Bedford OWB new to Highland Transport in 1944, one of a batch of four (15–18) with twenty-eight-seat utility SMT bodies, the other three receiving second-hand Duple-design bodies from SMT Bedford OBs FFS856–75. Based in Caithness, C17 ran from John O'Groats to Wick for the last two years, before being sold to Thomas MacDonald of Howmore in South Uist in February 1964. It was photographed on a Sunday in June 1968 in North Boisdale, returning from Our Lady of Sorrows church at Garrynamonie.

Bottom: MacAulay of Lochboisdale also ran on South Uist, and KGB265 is en route from Ludaig on the same day. Acquired from MacBrayne, it was licensed in July 1967 and withdrawn by August 1972, when it was twenty years old; it lay derelict at Ardivachar in June 1977. One of twenty-two Bedford OLAZs with a twenty-five-seat Duple Sportsman body, it was new in September 1952 and never had a mail compartment, although it had operated in Uist for much of its life. Transferred locally from Lochmaddy in North Uist to Lochboisdale in August 1963, it remained there until sold in March 1967.

Top: The fleet of R. & A. Cowe of Tobermory consisted of six Bedfords, three of which were OBs that had not been re-bodied and were not operated by MacBrayne. Of the remainder, only FFS871 returned to Mull immediately, being used principally on tours. A solitary twenty-seater Bedford OLAZ with a mail compartment, KGD907 arrived after the takeover for the service to Gruline. Originally on Skye, it had moved to North Uist in August 1962 to cover repairs to others of the same batch. Leaving Mull in January 1966, it returned north to operate the Glenelg–Kyle service, before being sold to Kyleakin Coaches on Skye in July.

Middle: A surprise arrival on Mull in June 1964, a month after MacBrayne had taken over, was KGE541, a twelve-year-old Albion from South Uist, which replaced 375FGB, a two-year-old Bedford VAS with a Duple Bella Vista body; it was sent over to the island immediately, but was soon required for the extended tours programme that summer. It remained at Tobermory until withdrawn in December 1965, and is parked on the pier on a Saturday in September 1964, having operated the morning service to Gruline.

Bottom: The last Commer to be withdrawn from the MacBrayne fleet was GGB617, based on Islay, in May 1965, three years after its contemporaries. Latterly, it had been delicensed during the winter, and was kept as a spare bus in the garage on Port Askaig pier, where it was photographed a month before finally leaving the island. It had been due to transfer to Mull the previous year, but this never took place. New in 1949 with a twenty-nine-seat Croft body, unlike similar FGG636 and GGE14, which had mail compartments, it was employed on tours and hires rather than on the connecting ferry services.

The ferry from West Loch Tarbert to Islay arrived at Port Ellen and Port Askaig on alternate days, and the mail bus assigned to this service was garaged so as to avoid dead mileage. On Monday, Wednesday and Friday, the bus left PA at 7.30 a.m. to connect with the ferry departure from PE at 8.50, and from PE on the other weekdays to connect with the sailing from PA. Waiting on the pier at Port Ellen for the 4 p.m. departure, in May 1965, are YYS174 for Port Askaig, and 385FGB for Portnahaven, both of which, despite their differing body styles, have mail compartments.

Vehicular access to Mull was through the port of Tobermory, until government funding was obtained to introduce three car ferries in 1964, in order to increase tourism in the Highlands and Islands. The last of these to be inaugurated was from Oban to Craignure, a shorter forty-five-minute crossing, allowing bus connections south to Fionnphort run by local operator Bowman, and north to Tobermory by MacBrayne, who had just started their bus operation on the island. UGB137H is sitting on Craignure pier, filling with passengers off MV *Columba*, ready to depart on the 12.15 service to Tobermory.

Although only three years old in August 1972, UGB137H, about to leave Craignure, already appears in need of a repaint. Taken over with the Mull operation by Highland Omnibuses in November 1971, becoming CD89, it would be painted in to their poppy-red and peacock-blue colours in two months' time. One of only two forty-seater Bedford SB5s with Willowbrook bodies to enter service with MacBrayne, it was immediately allocated to Tobermory, remaining on the island until Highland Omnibuses closed the depot on 4 April 1976, and sold their operation to Bowman.

Before 1973, the inhabitants of Lochaline on the Morvern peninsula in the remote area of Ardnamurchan, the most westerly point on the British mainland, only had access to Mull when the *Columba* called en route from Oban to Craignure. However, in April 1973, a new fifteen-minute ferry crossing was introduced from Lochaline to Fishnish on the east coast of Mull, halfway between Craignure and Tobermory. UGB137H, now in Highland livery, has arrived on the newly constructed pier at Fishnish on 14 May, operating the 5.15 service from Craignure to Tobermory.

The other two car ferries introduced in 1964 connected Skye (Armadale) with the mainland (Mallaig), and also North Uist (Lochmaddy) and Harris (Tarbert) with Uig in the north of the island. Collecting passengers for Portree and beyond from MV *Hebrides*, which has just arrived at Uig from Lochmaddy, is ex-MacBrayne AYS734B, a Bedford VAS new in June 1964 with a Duple Midland twenty-eight-seat body; it passed to Highland Omnibuses in May 1970, becoming CD55. Although painted in to fleet livery in May 1971, three months later it has still to receive a destination screen.

The ubiquitous 'bus group' sticker says Portree, but CD55 would continue to Kyleakin with connections at Portree. Having operated from Fort William since new, being the regular vehicle on the Mallaig–Arisaig service for the first three years of its life, its stay on Skye was short. It was withdrawn a year later, and sold through the dealer S&N, passing on to a number of English operators. Parked on the pier at Uig beside it is former MacBrayne Bedford OYS113F, with a Duple Bella Vista body, now Midland MW305 at Stepps depot, on an extended tour to the Western Isles.

Three years later, ex-MacBrayne 375FGB, now Highland Omnibuses CD43, awaits passengers from the same ferry, having been painted in to Highland's coach livery at the same time as CD55. As part of the MacBrayne extended tour fleet, it operated from Glasgow from when new in May 1962 until transferred to Portree in May 1968, passing to Highland Omnibuses in September 1970. Remaining on the island for tours and private hires until April 1976, it moved to Inverness to join the 'pool', and was sold a year later to the dealer S&N, appearing with Carruthers of New Abbey a month later.

A further year on and the ex-MacBrayne Bedfords are being replaced by full-size vehicles cascaded from the mainland, such as CD36 (GST953F), one of six Bedford VAM70 chassis with Willowbrook forty-one-seat dual-purpose bodies delivered in the blue coach livery in 1968, and initially used on tours. After two years in Wick, where it proved unreliable on service work, it arrived on Skye in August 1974. Although photographed operating the 8.35 a.m. service from Uig to Portree in July 1975, it spent most of its time on the island parked at Broadford for a school run, returning to Inverness in May 1979.

Top: Of the four Bedfords taken over with John Morrison's operation in Harris in June 1970, only two were operated by Highland Omnibuses, and only one painted in to Highland colours. Bedford SB3 TVA815, with a Plaxton forty-one-seat body, was the newest, having entered service with Gorman of Rutherglen in 1959, before passing to Lanarkshire operator Rae of Waterloo in 1961. It moved up to Harris in May 1968, and was regularly used on the service from Northton to Tarbert, and on to Stornoway. On 1 July 1968, it is arriving at Tarbert on the 3.00 service from Stornoway.

Middle: Given fleet number CD77 by Highland, it was refurbished and painted in to fleet livery in February 1971. Its worn-out dual-purpose seats were replaced by thirty-nine low back seats out of withdrawn ex-Western SMT Guy Arab LUFs. The plan was for it to be used on a school contract in North Uist, which required a big bus, from August 1971, but it had only reached Skye by then, being used on the inter-ferry service during the busy summer period. Approaching the Armadale turn off, it has left Broadford on the 8.35 a.m. service from Uig, duplicated by ex-MacBrayne Bedford EGA833C.

Bottom: During its rebuild, the boot of CD77 was modified, and it sits on the pier at Uig ready for its 8.35 departure. However, it did reach Lochmaddy later in the year, and passed to MacCuish of Sollas in January 1972, as, unlike the other MacBrayne island operations, those on North and South Uist were not taken over by Highland, but transferred to local independent operators. Also awaiting passengers is Scottish Omnibuses ZB104A, due to depart on the weekly service to Edinburgh, one of six thirty-eight-seat AECs intended for Highland, but four Fords acquired with the Starks fleet went north instead.

Top: Two full-size Bedfords from the Aviemore allocation were transferred to Skye when the MacBrayne operation passed to Highland Omnibuses in September 1970. The older was a 1961 SB1 model JJS17 with a Duple Super Vega forty-one-seat body, new to MacKenzie of Garve, who used it primarily on tours from Ullapool and Gairloch, and private hires. It was acquired with his business by Highland Omnibuses in October 1964, numbered CD9, and initially painted in to the cream and red livery, being repainted in to the two-tone blue livery in April 1966 and then transferred to Thurso.

Middle: Still largely confined to tour work, after two years it transferred back to Inverness for a further year, and when it reached Portree was still rarely used on service work until repainted again in March 1973, this time in to the poppy-red and peacock-blue bus livery, and fitted for OMO operation. It was then used intensively for the next two years, and awaits departure from Uig pier on 11 August 1973 at 8.35 a.m. On this occasion forty-nine-seat Leopard ZH542A will depart for Edinburgh, changing over with the similar ZH441A, arriving at 6.45 p.m., as the Highland vehicle AEC Reliance BA20 (LUS524E) lies unfit in Edinburgh.

Bottom: By 1975 it was the regular bus outstationed at Dunvegan for the service to Portree via Edinbane, which MacBrayne acquired from Peter Carson in April 1970, a month before the Skye operation was taken over by Highland Omnibuses. After leaving Skye at the end of the summer season, CD9 returned to join the pool at Inverness, being delicensed in December 1975. It lay at the depot in Needlefields for a further six months before sale to the dealer Ensign at Hornchurch, and was next seen with AA Lewington of Harold Hill in February 1978, being used as a source of spares.

Top: The local service from Portree to Uig was operated by Alisdair MacLeod, based in the small village of Duntulm at the northern extremity of the Trotternish Peninsula, the terminus being 2 miles further on at Kilmaluag. At the bus stance in Portree is twenty-five-seat SMT-bodied Bedford OB BWG247, new to W. Alexander in July 1948 as W232. It was transferred to Highland with their Inverness operation in 1952, becoming C173, latterly allocated to Caithness. Sold to MacLeod in April 1962, it was parked up, delicensed, at Duntulm by August 1964, still in the livery of Highland Omnibuses.

Middle: Another Bedford OB acquired from Highland, SX7039, had a longer life with MacLeod, arriving in June 1968 and still running in November 1973. Never operated by Highland or given a fleet number, it passed straight to MacLeod from Kennedy of Kiltarlity, who ran from Glenconvinth in to Inverness. New to McCabe of Winchburgh in 1950, it passed to MacKenzie of Dalry and on to Robert Kennedy by April 1961. By comparison, parked beside it in August 1971, is CD69, with mail compartment, on its regular service to Kilmaluag via the east side of the Trotternish Peninsula and the village of Staffin.

Bottom: Although MacBrayne operated the service network on Islay, providing ferry and airport connections, Royal Mail collection, shoppers' services, church runs, tours on a Tuesday and Thursday, private hires, and funeral attendances, the school services were all operated by J&H Caskie of Bowmore. Operating a fleet of Bedfords, usually obtained second-hand from Gold Line of Dunoon, and continuing with their elegant livery, they also ran tours and an airport service. SB7611, a twenty-seven-seat Bedford OB acquired in 1959, is seen leaving Port Ellen on the morning school run to Bowmore.

Top: The last Bedford OB in John Morrison's fleet, GDK852, with a twenty-seven-seat Duple body, seen here near Leverburgh, is on a Sunday run from Seilebost to Scarister church in August 1967. Nearby, thirty-eight-seat Plaxton-bodied Bedford SBG FYJ847 is operating the church run from Northton to Leverburgh. The OB was new to Yelloway Motor Services of Rochdale in July 1949, passing to Smith of Contin near Dingwall in 1960, and on to Morrison in August 1963. Withdrawn in July 1968, it was still lying at their garage in Northton four years later.

Middle: The service from Tarbert to Stornoway, taken over from John Mitchell of Stornoway, required full-size vehicles for its daytime runs in the summer, often with a duplicate in June and September. The 5.45 p.m. departure from Tarbert which arrived back at 9.40 was usually operated by GDK852, but in the winter, particularly when there was snow on the roads, the OB appeared on every journey. On such a day on 3 February 1968 it has arrived at Stornoway at 1.15, having operated through from Northton, which it left at 9.30 after its morning school run from Luskentyre to Leverburgh.

Bottom: By the time Bedford OB FFS877 was photographed at Garrabost on the Eye Peninsula in Lewis in November 1967, it was a mobile shop. Its last owner was John Murdo Morrison of Gravir, who operated a service from Lemreway to Stornoway via Gravir on alternate days with John MacMillan of Lemreway. Highland Omnibuses had acquired it in February 1957 from Scottish Omnibuses, who first licensed it in March 1948 numbered C177. As C23, Highland operated it latterly from Inverness depot, and sold it in November 1961.

Top: Two of the Bedford OWBs acquired by Highland Omnibuses with the operation of Macrae & Dick, in February 1952, had their original austerity Duple bodies re-bodied by Burlingham in November 1953. AST933 (C122) was used on tours, latterly from Dingwall depot, and sold to an operator in South Uist, MacLeod Brothers at Loch Skipport, in January 1964 for a school run to Iochdar primary school. Withdrawn in June 1968, it later achieved fame by becoming the iconic 'shell bus' owned by a Mrs Johnstone at Iochdar, who bought it as a non-runner to provide a 'spare room'.

Middle: Nearby at Howmore is FFS856, also re-bodied by Burlingham and acquired from Highland along with FFS858 in November 1964. New to Scottish Omnibuses in 1947 as C156 with a Duple body, it passed to Highland in January 1962. Parked beside it is another Bedford OB, AS1930 with a thirty-seat Duple body, newly acquired from Grant of Fort Augustus. Withdrawn are eleven-seat Morris 76BUS, and FVH411, a Bedford SB new to Hanson of Huddersfield in April 1952 with a thirty-three-seat Duple Vega body, and acquired from McLennan of Spittalfield in November 1962, after only three months with the company.

Bottom: Not all the re-bodied OBs in the Scottish Omnibuses fleet went to Highland, and eight of the twenty were sold to other operators, including Alexander MacPhee of Lochboisdale in South Uist, who acquired FFS873 in June 1962, and used it on a Sunday run from Lochboisdale to St Peter's church at Daliburgh. It was withdrawn by August 1971. Parked beside it is MacBrayne Duple Bella Vista AYS735B, up on an extended tour and providing transport to the local churches. It was transferred in October 1970 to Midland when the MacBrayne fleet was dispersed, but was not operated.

Top: Willie Sutherland of Carbost obtained his vehicles from Highland Omnibuses, who regularly painted them for him before they left for Skye. This became an annual event, and FFS866, one of the twelve Bedfords with Burlingham 'baby' Seagull bodies acquired by Highland in January 1962, arrived on the island in December 1964, and regularly appeared on the Portree–Portnalong and Glenbrittle services over the next three years. As C16 it had operated for Highland from Inverness depot, and surprisingly was used on a variety of services, including duplicate and all day runs to Nairn and Dingwall.

Middle: Appearing at Portree bus stance in the same period was FFS860, which retained its Highland livery while in the fleet of MacLeod of Duntulm. As C10 with Highland, its fleet number matched the registration number. The only one of the batch not to do so was FFS867, which became C21, although C11 never ran for the company, as it sustained accident damage on delivery. While with Highland, it was allocated to Caithness, working out of Dunbeath depot on a school contract from Berriedale to Lybster. Withdrawn in February 1965, it ran on Skye for three years, ending up as a shed on the island.

Bottom: Another vehicle from that batch of re-bodied SMT Bedford OBs to end up in the islands was FFS871, sold to Locke, the Edinburgh dealer, in March 1962, then passing on to R&A Cowe. It arrived at Tarbert in September 1966 to replace Bedford OLAZ KGB262, which had only been on Harris for four months. Parked beside it in the depot is another vehicle acquired with the Tobermory operation, RGD753, fleet number L7, a Ford lorry, one of four based on the island at that time. Unfortunately I can't identify the coach beside it, as this slide was one never returned by the dealer to whom I had lent it.

Parked on the pier at Tarbert, waiting to take up an island tour, FFS871 was primarily allocated to Harris for this purpose. At the beginning of the tourist season, it was employed on Wallace Arnold tours. It was also available for private hires and funerals, and acted as a spare bus for the two school services, although the eleven-seat Ford NST683 could cover the run to Maruig. The Sunday Communion service, however, was operated by a twenty-eight-seat Bedford C5Z, WGG625, which remained on the island until Highland Omnibuses took over the services in June 1971.

The school contracts inherited from the Harris Hotel Garage were from Tarbert Academy to Maruig and Kyles of Scalpay, and FFS871 is returning from Kyles of Scalpay in September 1967. New in February 1948, with a twenty-five-seat SMT body to Duple design, it was re-bodied in 1953 and used on extended tours by Scottish Omnibuses. It remained on Harris until 14 June 1968, proving to be reliable and versatile, but was not replaced thereafter. When an extra coach was required, one came from North Uist on loan, usually Duple coach-bodied Bedford C5Z ESY89, also acquired from Cowe of Tobermory.

However, FFS871 had a further life ahead of it, this time on yet another island, because it crossed the Minch again, this time to the Isle of Skye. It had been acquired by the Free Presbyterian Church at Portree, and is photographed in Somerled Square in Portree in September 1968, where it frequently sat, and would meet up with the other vehicles of the same batch operating on Skye.

Looking unloved in its afterlife as a static caravan or bothy on the windswept 'Braes' on the road from Portree down to Peinchorran, it was photographed still intact in June 1971 when it was twenty-three years old. It was still there in 1989. However, its days were not over, as it was purchased by an enthusiast for preservation, and later passed in to the hands of Scarborough-based Bluebird Vehicles, a firm which builds minibuses, and carries out van conversions and coachwork refurbishment for Plaxton. At present its restoration is well underway, but in to what livery remains uncertain.

The other Bedford OWB from the Macrae & Dick fleet that Highland Omnibuses re-bodied was AST934 (C123), which, like its sister AST933, was latterly used on tours from Dingwall depot. It, however, lasted a year longer, being withdrawn in November 1964. It was acquired by John Morrison of Northton two months later, and continued to operate in Highland colours. By May 1968 it had moved north to Lewis, and was now in use as a mobile shop owned by Kenneth Mclennan at Arnol, where it was photographed well stocked with a wide selection of groceries and other items.

It was common to find withdrawn buses in various guises throughout the islands, and Bedford OB XS6564 is lying dilapidated and no doubt cannibalised in a yard near Marybank outside Stornoway. Latterly it had operated for Hebridean Transport, who had acquired it from Western SMT via Millburn Motors, to whom it was sold in 1954. New to Young's Bus Service of Paisley in February 1949 with a Duple twenty-nine-seat body, it passed to Western SMT in January 1951, becoming JB2184 at Johnstone depot, and was painted in the black and white coach livery.

Top: Parked in a field at Uachdar on Benbecula is a caravan converted from Austin CST535, which was last licensed as a PSV with MacDonald of Howmore in February 1963. As part of the twenty-seven-vehicle fleet of Macrae & Dick, it passed to Highland Omnibuses in February 1952, given fleet number D115, and was withdrawn in late 1955, moving to South Uist in February 1956. Its final allocation was in Caithness, where it was kept as a spare for a school contract at Mey.

Middle: An uncommon model, CST535 was an Austin CXB new in May 1948 with a twenty-six-seat body by Walker of Aberdeen, later having its seating capacity increased to twenty-eight. When I photographed it in August 1958, it was parked at the ferry terminal at Lochboisdale, having arrived in from Carnan at the north end of South Uist.

Bottom: Another unusual Austin that was no longer in use as a PSV was CES785, seen near Daliburgh in use as a mobile shop in July 1967. Surprisingly, it was still in the livery of its first owner, Colin Christison of Blairgowrie in Perthshire. An Austin model K4/CXB, it was new in March 1949 with a Mann Egerton twenty-nine-seat body, passing to A&C McLennan of Spittalfield in February 1960. In 1963 it was sold to MacDonald of Howmore and converted for its new use.

Top: Withdrawn vehicles were also scattered around Skye and other islands, and former Highland Omnibuses AEC Reliance LST503 (B9), which passed to Sutherland in May 1974, lies delicensed by the roadside near Carbost in August 1977. Parked in front of it is XGD775, still operating the Portree–Portnalong service. Also a Park Royal-bodied Reliance, but with Roe involvement to BET design, it had been new to MacBrayne in July 1959 for Fort William town services, but taken over by Highland, becoming B44, and fitted with a new front grille – a common practice – before moving to Skye in May 1976.

Middle: Parked beside XGD775 in the square at Portree, in a similar livery, is a Bedford SBO with a Duple Midland thirty-nine-seat body, LCJ929, belonging to Neil Beaton, who acquired it from Banstead Coaches in August 1969, and used it on a school run. Similar Bedfords, but fifteen years newer and with Willowbrook bodies, are Highland CD41/89 (UGB138/7H). The former was originally purchased for the Glendale–Portree via Dunvegan service by MacBrayne, and remained on the island until withdrawn in June 1981. However, on 11 April 1977, it has just arrived from Dunvegan via Sligachan.

Bottom: A third Willowbrook-bodied Bedford SB5 (NST175J) was ordered by MacBrayne, but arrived after the takeover, becoming CD75 painted in the red and blue livery. Allocated to the Foyers–Inverness service for the first six years of its life and then the Lairg–Golspie run until withdrawn, both of which had narrow roads, it paid a surprise overnight visit to Portree on 17 September 1976. CD41 had failed in Inverness, and the replacement Duple Viceroy-bodied Bedford was considered unsuitable. The next morning it is about to depart for Inverness, parked beside CD40 just in from Kilmaluag and CD35.

Top: CD89 arrived on Skye in April 1976, when Highland closed their Mull depot in Tobermory, and proved less reliable than CD41. It tended to be used as an occasional school bus, either outstationed at Broadford for the contract from Kyleakin, or in the school holidays parked up at Dunvegan. By April 1981, it is sitting at Portree out of use, as the door is manually operated. Further along is CD28 (GST501), fitted with a power-operated door from new and transferred from Oban in June 1977 to operate the Braes service. It left Skye in October 1981, and was sold to Kennedy of Orinsay on Lewis.

Middle: CD75, based in Dornoch, was withdrawn in April 1981, and by 27 June both CD41 and 89 were delicensed at Inverness where they lay until October. Both were now in their third livery, having been painted in to the poppy-red and grey livery the previous year. Parked delicensed beside them is Albion Lowlander AL41 (BCS256C), ex-Western SMT KN1923 down from Dingwall, and later preserved. On the other side withdrawn is forty-nine-seat AEC Reliance BA13 (EWS137D), new to Scottish Omnibuses in November 1966, transferred to Highland in December 1969, and outstationed at Fort Augustus.

Bottom: In October 1981, both CD41 and CD89 were sold to McDonald of Back in Lewis, where they operated on his service from Tolsta to Stornoway. CD89 was withdrawn after sustaining front-end damage in an accident on the premises in 1986, and CD41 was taken out of service in late 1988. Both vehicles were still at the depot when I visited ten years later, and CD41 is in the process of being restored at the moment by the Western Isles Transport Preservation Group.

The Bedford SB5 was the most common bus to be seen in Lewis throughout the 1960s, with Mitchell and Hebridean Transport operating twenty, which were purchased new. In 1967, three arrived within six months, EJS700–900E, and EJS700E is seen in August having left the airport for the bus station on its regular schedule; it is passing JJS444, heading for Melbost, deputising for the regular EJS222D. Both vehicles were licensed to 'Western Lewis Coaches', 70 Bayhead Street, Stornoway, which was associated with John Mitchell (Stornoway) Ltd of the same address.

A year later and EJS222D has turned off the Point road on the local service from Marybank to Melbost, where it is parked at night. New in 1966 with a Duple Midland forty-two-seat body like the other Bedford SB5s running on Lewis, it was withdrawn in 1980. The other Stornoway town service from Plasterfield to Newmarket was operated by similar DJS600D, new in March 1966 and actually licensed to John Mitchell. It was parked at Laxdale overnight. The other licensed services were from Port of Ness to Stornoway, North Tolsta and Back to Stornoway, and the Carloway Circular.

In the previous picture, JJS444 was in the pale blue version of the livery, and was the last to be repainted in to dark blue with a cream band, the transformation being well underway when it was photographed on 28 May 1968. Its next livery change was in to the red and cream colours of Lochs Motor Transport in June 1973. New in June 1961 with JJS333, it was followed a year later by identical KJS555 and KJS666, after which the registrations had year suffixes, but with numbers that were numerically significant. JJS333 also went to Lochs Motor Transport, but only as a source of spares.

There were seven journeys from Back to and from Stornoway, and KJS555 is on the 5.30 p.m. service from Stornoway, letting off its passengers in Back in August 1968. It would return to Stornoway at 7.20 for a 9.30 departure, and back again for the last run at 11.00, being parked at Lower Back overnight. It shared the duties with KJS666, parked at Upper Back overnight, and they also operated Sunday church runs from Tong and Gress respectively. KJS555 passed to the Nicolson Institute in 1969, and KJS666 to Galson Motor Services, who kept it at Ness for a school contract.

Top: The last of the six vehicles purchased by Hebridean Transport from Hutchison of Overtown was OVA764 which is parked at Upper Bayble on 10 June 1968, having operated the 6 p.m. service from Stornoway. A Bedford SBO new in February 1957, with the usual Duple Midland forty-two-seat body and a manually operated door, it was by then the oldest Bedford in the fleet. Purchased from Hutchison in 1959, it was followed by the similar PVA196 the following year; however, this bus was sold on after only six years on Lewis.

Middle: In April 1970, OVA764 passed on to Lochs Motor Transport, who operated it for five years and replaced it with a similar vehicle from the fleet of Hebridean Transport, JJS628. Having arrived at its stance in Stornoway on a Saturday in August 1972, it is about to return to Ranish at 9 a.m., with further journeys at 1.15, 6.15 and the late run at 11 p.m. Although devoid of a destination screen or board, this would have been superfluous, as its passengers knew the driver, the vehicle and the bus stop where it was sitting.

Bottom: Hebridean Transport was the sole operator of services on the Eye Peninsula, with journeys to Swordale, Lower and Upper Bayble and Portnaguran. AJS296B was a Bedford SB13 new in 1964, and spent all its life running with the one operator, being cannibalised for spare parts in 1979. It was photographed in August 1967 at Sheshader Road end, returning to Stornoway on the 3.50 service from Portnaguran. It departed again at 6.5 p.m. to Sheshader, and stayed overnight at Portnaguran.

Top: Although many of the vehicles in the fleet of Hebridean Transport were parked at or near the drivers' houses overnight, as with John Mitchell's buses, the depot was in Stornoway, at Inaclete Road. Parked outside in June 1968 are OVA764 and Albion NVD203. Passing by is Bedford RVA407 in the livery of Hebridean Transport, but in fact it is no longer in their fleet and is now running with Galson Motor Services, being replaced in the Hebridean fleet by HJS519G.

Middle: Five months later, RVA407 has been painted in to the livery of Galson Motor Services, and has arrived at Stornoway on the 12.30 service from Port of Ness, at present being the spare bus kept at Barvas. It had left Hebridean Transport in April after a relatively short time in their fleet, having been acquired from Hutchison of Overtown, who themselves had only kept it for eleven months, in January 1959.

Bottom: Hebridean Transport had acquired three Albion Victor FT39AL models with thirty-five-seat Duple coach bodies from Hutchison, of which two, bought in 1959, LVD635 and LVD891, were withdrawn five years later. NVD203, however, came in February 1958, but was not sold until November 1971, to Kennedy of Orinsay. Lying at Lochs Motor Transport depot at Leurbost in August 1973, it was still in Hebridean colours. Seen here at Upper Bayble off the 6.00 service from Stornoway, it is passing my car, a battered standard 1962 Mini deceptively fitted with a 1100 cc engine tuned for rally driving.

Top: The Hebridean Transport buses left from stances in a big open area, and four Bedfords are waiting for the teatime departures in August 1967. HJS65 will depart at 6.00 to Upper Bayble; CJS344C for Swordale, being parked at Knock overnight; and at 6.5 p.m. AJS296B acts as a duplicate to Sheshader for KJS817, which continues to Portnaguran, where it remains overnight. KJS817 and HJS65 are in the livery with the darker roof. HJS65 retained this livery until sold, and when I photographed it with Economic Forestry, near Hairmyres Hospital at East Kilbride in 1973, its livery was unchanged.

Middle: Six years later, CJS344C is soon to leave the bus stance at 3.30 for Lower Bayble. New in July 1965, it was sold as an NPSV in 1979. Parked beside it is MJS113J, a forty-seat Willowbrook-bodied Bedford SB5 new in March 1971, but to the same design as the forty-two-seat Duple Midland-bodied Bedfords in the fleet. It had replaced the non-standard Albion NVD203, and had arrived at 2.55 from Swordale to depart again at 4.30 for Portnaguran, where it would later be parked overnight.

Bottom: Looking across at the bus station in Cromwell Street, from which the buses of John Mitchell departed, AJS111B, parked overnight at Low Tolsta, is leaving for Tolsta on the 1.00 service, and will arrive back at Stornoway at 2.45. New in June 1964, it was withdrawn in 1978 and ended up as a builder's hut at Back. Although the service to Tarbert and Northton, operated by Western Lewis Coaches, no longer left from this bus station when Morrison of Northton took over, Highland Omnibuses used it when they acquired the route in June 1970.

Top: DJS600D had been allocated to the local service from Newmarket to Plasterfield from its arrival in March 1966, having replaced a twin-steer Bedford VAL. AJS110B, and is parked at the bus station between runs in August 1971. While the bus station looks relatively empty mid-morning, it could be very busy in the late afternoon, and on Saturday when many families came in from more distant parts of the island.

Middle: Saturdays in the tourist season could be particularly busy and, in August 1973, PJS10L, a Bedford SB5 with a forty-two-seat Willowbrook body new in September 1972, has arrived at the bus station on the airport service. Parked in front is BJS999C on the local service to Melbost. New in September 1965, it was withdrawn in 1979 and ended up as a store at Arnol. In the background is Highland Omnibuses CD66 (HGA977D), up from Harris and due to depart on the 3.30 service to Tarbert.

Bottom: Just arrived in on the circular service from Callanish and Carloway is AJS111B, now allocated to this route, which is licensed to Western Lewis Coaches with the bus outstationed at Brue. Arriving in the morning via Achmore, and returning at 5.30, it also departs at 12.30, doing a clockwise circular tour and arriving back at Stornoway at 2.45. Also now arrived at the bus station is EJS700E, which will depart at 3.00 for Newmarket.

Top: Both Galson Motor Services and John Morrison of Northton parked their buses on an open area along from the harbour, and usually operated them in the livery in which they were acquired. Beside Bedfords KWY559 and SJH717 from the Galson fleet is Morrison's FYJ847, a Bedford SBG with a thirty-eight-seat Plaxton body, new in 1957 to Dickson of Dundee. Becoming Highland Omnibuses CD78 in June 1970, it was withdrawn in August 1971 and sold to Allander coaches of Milngavie in April 1972; they operated it still in the livery of Hunter of Loanhead, who had sold it to Morrison back in May 1967.

Middle: Although Mitchell keeps a vehicle at Ness with a similar schedule to the one at Brue, incorporating a midday return journey, the principal operator is Galson Motor Services of Barvas, which runs a mixed fleet of Bedfords, all acquired second-hand. EJS483 was a Bedford SB1 new to Mitchell in 1958, passing to Galson MS in April 1969 to replace WMV418. Kept at Barvas, it has arrived at its bus stance in Stornoway on the 5.30 service from Ness. Parked behind is ex-MacBrayne Bedford VAS TUS349G, now Midland MW308Ss, up on an extended tour in 1973. It was not withdrawn until 1977.

Bottom: In August 1973, Galson Motor Services replaced SJH717 with 701RDH, a Bedford SB8 with a forty-one-seat Duple Super Vega body, acquired through the dealer S&N of Bishopbriggs. Still in the livery of its previous owner, Grangeburn Coaches of Motherwell, it has arrived at Stornoway on 15 August 1975 on the 12.30 service from Ness, where it is kept overnight for a school contract in the morning to Shader.

Top: Parked nearby is Albion Viking BWG650B of Lochs MS, the regular vehicle on the Stornoway–Ranish service. Parked in the distance are Duple Midland-bodied Bedford SB8 JJS628, previously with Hebridean Transport, which replaced Dodge 3033PE on its school contract, and similar JJS444, acquired from John Mitchell, due to operate a school contract to Callanish. In the foreground is 777DGB, a Bedford VAS previously with Glasgow City Council, now in service with Kennedy of Orinsay, who operates in to Stornoway on a Tuesday, Thursday and Friday, and also Mondays in term time.

Middle: Albion Viking BWG650B was a demonstrator exhibited at the 1963 Scottish Motor Show in the blue and cream colours of W. Alexander & Sons (Midland) Ltd. It entered service in August 1964 at Perth depot, but was returned to Albion Motors in 1965 and sold to Barrie of Balloch, who used it on the service to Balmaha. In December 1967, it arrived on Lewis already converted for OMO operation, and was kept in a yard at Ranish overnight for the service to Stornoway. On the occasions when it would not start in the morning, Bedford SK6348 would come down to operate the first run at 7 a.m.

Bottom: In these pictures it is parked by Leurbost school to take pupils to Cameron Terrace, and return to Stornoway to depart at 4.15 for Ranish. Although unique, in that it was the only Albion Viking with a Leyland 370 vertical front engine, model VK41L, it was a robust and practical lightweight chassis and suited to the island roads. The standard-looking Alexander Y-type body had a luggage area on the nearside behind the passenger door, and accommodated forty-one seats. No other examples entered service in the UK, but the rear engine Albion Viking entered service with the Scottish Bus Group in 1965.

Another interesting Albion to operate in the islands was KGE541, shown here at the Albion Works before entering service with the Scottish Co-operative Wholesale Society Limited (Skye Transport Company) in Portree in October 1952. This was the last vehicle it purchased before being taken over by MacBrayne in November 1958. It was an Albion FT3AB with a rare body, built by Harvey Brothers of Strathaven, with twenty-three seats and a mail compartment, being one of only three bus bodies they built after the war, one for the Mauritius Government Railways and another for Falkirk Hospital Board. (Robert Grieves Collection)

MacBrayne rebuilt the body, removing the mail compartment and adding a row of red upholstered seats, although I never discovered what vehicle they came out of. It was first moved to Islay, where it had arrived by May 1960, and was allocated to the Portnahaven–Port Ellen/Port Askaig service, being garaged at Portnahaven overnight. By May 1962, it had moved to Lochboisdale in South Uist, where it was garaged overnight, and is photographed outside the depot. (Robert Grieves)

In June 1964, it moved yet again to a fourth island, Mull, where it remained until withdrawn in December 1965; it then left for the mainland and the Lancefield Street depot of MacBrayne in Glasgow. A rugged machine, it was eminently suited to the single-track roads and the rough terrain, and was effectively a spare bus on the island. In May 1966 it was purchased by Laidlaw, a contractor in Rutherglen, but I never saw it again, and never heard of its eventual fate.

When new, KGE541 had a six-cylinder petrol engine, but was converted to a diesel engine by MacBrayne, and these pictures, taken in September 1964, show it leaving the front at Tobermory on the 4.00 service to Gruline, and returning at 5.25 p.m., although it no longer had a destination blind fitted. It was extremely noisy as it growled its way up the steep hill, and appeared cumbersome as it cornered on its return journey, though it only weighed 3-14-2 tons. The rear end had clearly been modified at the time the mail compartment was removed.

Top: Another vehicle to be transferred to Mull at the takeover of Cowe's fleet was UGA616, MacBrayne's first Bedford C class with a truck chassis modified for PSV use, and the only C4 (4-ton) model to enter their fleet. New in May 1958 with a twenty-nine-seat Duple body, it was on North Uist by May 1962. After only a year on Mull, it left for Ardrishaig. Usually based at Lochgoilhead, often as a third spare bus, it sometimes ran the school contract via Hell's Glen to Inveraray. In the summer it was used on tours from Ardrishaig to Rothesay. Delicensed at Glasgow by January 1969, it was also sold to Laidlaw.

Middle: The other unique Bedford with this body in the MacBrayne fleet was ESY89, a C5 model acquired with the Cowe operation in May 1964, distinguished internally by its grey individual seats. New to Hunter of Loanhead in January 1958, it reached Mull by 1961. However, it never operated for MacBrayne there, and after repainting moved to Skye, replacing similar WGG545, the first C5 to enter the fleet, to North Uist. This was a familiar progression, as ESY89 itself also moved to North Uist in January 1966. It was photographed in the square at Portree in September 1964.

Bottom: While on North Uist, it was used as the spare bus for the Uists, and kept at Lochmaddy, as it was mechanically troublesome, and in July 1966 I found it down in Glasgow for repair. While on loan to Harris, as cover for WGG625, it failed, and both vehicles were photographed in the workshops at Tarbert on 13 April 1968. By June it was back on loan to Harris after FFS871 had left, as there was no longer a spare bus at Tarbert. In March 1970, it was withdrawn from service in North Uist, and moved to MacLeod of Loch Skipport in South Uist in September 1970, eventually being cannibalised.

Top: During this period WGG630 was also allocated to Harris, being used on the two school runs as well as tours and private hires, and in April 1968 it is parked outside the entrance to Lews Castle, Stornoway. Leaving the island in May 1971, a month before the formal takeover, MacBrayne replaced it with the similar WGG629 from North Uist, and in August Highland Omnibuses sold it to the Inverness County Council Education Department. In 1981 it entered preservation, and, restored to MacBrayne colours, it regularly appears at rallies and events all over the country.

Middle: Out of a fleet of twenty-two Bedford C5s with Duple coach bodies purchased by MacBrayne, only two had mail compartments, and both were delivered new to Islay. Distinguished by the additional area of red below the windows, 610CYS is parked at the depot at Port Ellen in May 1965 beside KGE420 (L3), an Austin lorry new in 1952. It operated on the island for almost eleven years until Highland Omnibuses took over in January 1972, but YYS174, which had just arrived at the depot on service from Port Askaig, left Islay in May 1966 after only six years on the island.

Bottom: YYS174 then spent the next five years based at Ardrishaig until Western SMT took over. Usually allocated to Lochgoilhead for the mail service from Carrick Castle to 'Top of the Rest and Be Thankful', it often seemed to be at Glasgow for repair, and was replaced by either UGA616, a Bedford VAS, or even, on 17 March 1970, by an eight-month-old tour coach, TGE201G. Parked beside YYS174 at Lochgoilhead garage in June 1966 is AYS736B for the school service through Hell's Glen to Inveraray, the bus returning to Butterbridge during the day to allow the driver to return as a passenger to Lochgilphead.

In October 1970, the Ardrishaig operation passed to Western SMT under the control of their Thornliebank depot, with the four Bedfords, YYS174 and VAS HGA985D, EGA834C and AYS736B becoming ME1–4. The Lochgoilhead school service was withdrawn in September 1971. Sitting outside Ardrishaig depot in March 1973 is YYS174, now in WSMT colours. Parked beside it is Highland Omnibuses AEC Reliance B76, still in the livery of Midland Scottish, in which fleet it was MAC193C at Crieff depot. It has arrived on the service from Oban, while ME2 has worked the run from Ardrishaig to Oban.

In June 1973, the Carrick Castle service passed to local businessman Douglas Campbell of Lochgoilhead, and YYS174 is sitting at the 'Top of the Rest' in July awaiting its connections. Thereafter it had an illustrious career, appearing in the long running soap *High Road*, as Maggie's bus (in Glendarroch), and still in Western livery turned up in Bearsden in May 1979 to take my children on school swimming pool trips. Later it was repainted in to MacBrayne livery in Kilmarnock using my slides as a guide, and operated with Stagecoach on Arran. It is now in private preservation.

When Maroner of Lochwinnoch, who operated the school contracts on Islay, lost them to Western SMT in May 1980, five fifty-five-seat Leopards, previously with Paton of Renfrew, arrived on the island to take over. Willowbrook-bodied YL6, nominally the spare bus but deputising for YL7, is at Bowmore on the 11.30 service from Port Ellen to Portnahaven, where it is parked at night. Becoming MPE435 when Midland took over in June 1985, it was due for transfer to Bannockburn depot, but it passed to Mundell with the Islay operation on 26 October 1986, and on to Clark at Banchory by November 1989. (Robert Grieves)

Gregor MacGregor was in charge of Western's operation on Islay, and is seen here cleaning YL7. Of the other three Duple-bodied vehicles, YL8 was normally kept at Bridgend, YL9 at Kells and YL10 at Bowmore. Becoming Midland MPE436–9, 436 and 437 were transferred to Larbert, with 437 receiving an Alexander fifty-three-seat body from Fife FPE62D in April 1987. 438 was transferred with 439 to Oban in August 1986 and outstationed at Easdale until it was burnt in the Oban depot fire in November 1990. 439 moved to Kelvin Central Buses in late 1990, becoming 1452 at Airbles depot. (Robert Grieves)

The MacBrayne operation on Islay passed to Highland Omnibuses in January 1972, with the three remaining buses on the island, 610CYS and two Bedford VAS with mail compartments – 385FGB and HGA983D, with a twenty-four-seat Willowbrook body, which had replaced YYS174. They became Highland C29, CD92 and 93, being the last of the MacBrayne fleet to be absorbed in to Highland Omnibuses. However, the Post Office took over these services on 1 October 1973 with three Commer post buses. In 1979, TSB341T is going to leave Bowmore for Port Ellen, and NSB336R for the airport. (Robert Grieves)

On Mull, the first run introduced by the Post Office was from Craignure to Lochbuie on 1 December 1972. DSF751L (3750009), an eleven-seat Commer converted by Rootes, and just transferred to replace the original vehicle allocated, BSC494L (2750007), is parked at Craignure in October 1973. It has arrived back at the pier at 12.37 after its daily four-hour journey, although on a Monday it has an additional run at 7.15 a.m. direct to Lochbuie. In August 1995, a further service was introduced between Salen and Burg via the Ulva Ferry, using a four-seat Ford Mondeo estate car, but it was withdrawn in 2005.

Top: MacBrayne Thornycroft FGE678 survived much longer than the rest of the batch, as it lived on as a mobile tours booking office until 1964. After passing through a number of owners, it is currently undergoing restoration in Basingstoke (the home of Thornycrofts) as a MacBrayne lorry, similar to FGE241, which became L4. New in January 1948 with a seven-seat Harkness body and mail compartment, it latterly operated on Skye, being withdrawn in 1960. It was parked in Portree square in September 1963 beside Nicolson of Skeabost Bridge twenty-seven-seat Kenex-bodied Ford UST25, new in 1962.

Middle: The other former MacBrayne Thornycroft to survive in to preservation is HGG359, new in July 1950 with a twenty-seat Croft body, the last of a batch of six, none of which had mail compartments. Garaged at Port Askaig in April 1959, it then moved to Lochgoilhead as the spare bus used on tours, and as a duplicate for the late Friday connection at 7.10 p.m. from Arrochar station to Carrick Castle. It was withdrawn in May 1962, and sold the following month to MacLachlan of Tayvallich, with whom it was photographed in November 1968 en route to Lochgilphead, despite the destination.

Bottom: The other small vehicle purchased at that time that was considered suitable for the rough roads and ferry landings was the Commer Commander (three were rebuilt ex-WD Q4 chassis), and fifteen were delivered in 1948/9, all with Croft bodies. Four had mail compartments (three with twenty seats, one with twenty-five), and the remainder had twenty-nine seats. FGG637 was new in April 1948 with a twenty-seat body and mail compartment, and was based in South Uist in August 1958 when I visited. It was photographed in Lochboisdale loading up for Balivanich and Gramsdale. It was sold for scrap in December 1960. (Robert Grieves)

In 1968, MacAulay Brothers of Lochboisdale operated a school service from South Boisdale to Daliburgh in addition to the Sunday church run. Ex-MacBrayne Bedford OLAZ KGB265 is parked at Lochboisdale, with the legal details of the owner unusually displayed on the offside of the bus. It was to be the first of many ex-MacBrayne buses they would operate, as the licences for the MacBrayne operation in South Uist were transferred direct to MacAulay Brothers in January 1972, although the actual operation changed hands in November 1971. It ended up derelict at Ardivachar.

The services transferred were the main inter-island route from Lochboisdale in South Uist to Lochmaddy in North Uist, connecting the main ferry terminals and the airport at Balivanich; a school service from South Glendale to Lochboisdale; and a Sunday service from Parkview to the Church of Scotland at Griminish on Benbecula. The other operator in Lochboisdale was Alexander MacPhee, who operated ex-Scottish Omnibuses Bedford OB FFS873, still in acquired livery on a school run from Stoneybridge to Daliburgh, and photographed passing MacAulay's KGB265.

By the time that MacBrayne transferred these licences to MacAuley Brothers, there were only three buses based in Lochboisdale, 378–9/83FGB, all Bedford VAS new in 1962 with thirty-seat Duple Midland bodies, and all three passed to MacAulay Brothers. A further similar vehicle, EGA828C, new in May 1965 with twenty-nine seats, arrived from Highland Omnibuses in November 1974. Delivered new to Inverness, it was outstationed at Glenurquhart, and remained so when Highland Omnibuses took over in April 1970, being numbered CD60, until replaced in September 1972 when it joined the pool until it was sold. (Robert Grieves)

Two further ex-MacBrayne Bedfords arrived when the licences were transferred, having joined the Highland fleet from the MacBrayne operation in Mull when it was acquired in November 1971. These were C5 models YYS178 and 180, with twenty-nine-seat Duple coach bodies, given fleet numbers C26 and 27 in the Highland fleet. YYS178 was new in April 1960, and had moved from Fort William to Kinlochleven in September 1963 as a spare bus, and then on to Mull in May 1964 when the Cowe fleet was taken over, for tours and also the Gruline service. It was derelict at Ardmore in South Uist in May 1979. (Robert Grieves)

Top: Of the MacBrayne Bedfords passed directly to MacAulay Brothers, 378FGB had arrived on South Uist from Fort William in May 1964, in a complicated vehicle exchange that allowed YYS179 to move to North Uist to replace UGA616, which was transferred to Mull. The main route operated from Lochboisdale was north to Benbecula and Lochmaddy in North Uist, and it is on the 8.50 a.m. summer service to Balivanich airport, with the generic destination on the screen. If it had been a Wednesday or Friday, it would have connected with a service to Lochmaddy via Carinish.

Middle: On a Sunday, there were two church runs operated from Lochboisdale garage, from Loch Eynort area to St Mary's church at Bornish, and from Lochboisdale to St Peter's church at Daliburgh. In addition, the coach that was up on the extended tour also took those passengers who so wished to church. Here, 383FGB, which also passed to MacAulay Brothers, is leaving Lochboisdale Pier for Daliburgh. New to Inverness, where it was outstationed at Whitebridge, it arrived on South Uist in May 1965 to replace Bedford OLAZ KGD267, and was withdrawn from the MacAulay fleet in early 1980.

Bottom: A further MacBrayne bus that passed direct to an island operator with the route it operated was the similar 380FGB, acquired by MacLean of Grimsay in North Uist with the Lochmaddy–Baleloch circle on 29 January 1972. Two years later it moved south to join the fleet of MacDonald of Howmore. It was allocated to Lochmaddy in May 1962 when new, to replace a Thornycroft HGG358, and usually operated the through service from Lochmaddy to Lochboisdale. Here it is parked at Claddach, where it is based for the school run from Grimsay to Bayhead, and the Baleloch circle, which connects with the boat.

Top: In contrast to the Uists, the vehicles which operated on Islay usually had mail compartments. However, both EGA833C, which had arrived new in May 1965 to replace Commer GGB617, and HGA979D, which came in 1966 to replace Bedford OLAZ KGD904 (which had a mail compartment), did not. However, latterly they were both delicensed during the winter period, and EGA833C was not replaced when it left for Fort William in June 1969; nor was HGA979D, which went to North Uist in May 1971. Bedford 385FGB, however, did have a mail compartment, and is at Bridgend en route for Portnahaven.

Middle: The Portnahaven service appeared to be allocated a more basic vehicle, and 385FGB had arrived new in May 1962 to replace Albion KGE541 (which had itself replaced Commer GGG14). It remained on the service for its entire life, until September 1972 when it was withdrawn and replaced by HGA976D from Fort William. Numbered CD92, but never repainted in to Highland colours, it was sold to a contractor. Here it is passing the garage at Portnahaven, which originally was a three-sided 'shed' with no roof and no front door! It remains to this day with the 'MacBraynes' still visible.

Bottom: Returning from Portnahaven at 1.15, 385FGB has arrived at Port Ellen and is sitting on the pier, due to return at 4.30, while YYS174 will make the connecting journey to Port Askaig. Of the three vehicles that remained on the island when Highland took over – 385FGB, 610CYS and HGA983D – all had been replaced before the operation was given up: 610CYS by EGA832C from Mull, and HGA983D by similar HGA981D from Skye.

Historically, MacBrayne kept a single bus in this garage at Port Charlotte, latterly Bedford OLAZ KGD904, which had replaced Thornycroft HGG359 when it moved to Lochgoilhead. Both vehicles subsequently ran for MacLachlan of Tayvallich, and are now preserved. KGD904 was used for private hires, funerals, WRI outings, Sunday evening church runs, and transport to island shows, and, when required, acted as a duplicate to the Portnahaven bus, heading for Port Ellen or Port Askaig. The similar KGE243, with only fourteen seats, was kept at Port Ellen for tours, but delicensed during the winter.

The MacBrayne garage at Lochboisdale easily accommodated the three vehicles finally allocated to it, and 383FGB is entering to join 378FGB and 379FGB, already parked inside. The latter had moved down from North Uist in 1967, having been transferred there from Skye a year earlier, and was the first of the three to be withdrawn by MacAulay in 1979. It was, however, never formally scrapped, and ended up buried under the office of the new depot. In 1962 there were still five buses garaged here, including Albion KGE541 and Plaxton-bodied Commer HDG765, both unique in the MacBrayne fleet.

The MacBrayne North Uist base was at Lochmaddy, but there was also a bus kept at Claddach and one at Grenitote. Latterly only one was needed at Lochmaddy for the service to South Uist, and usually there was a spare bus too. By August 1971, changes were about to occur. 378FGB has arrived from Lochboisdale, changing over with Lochmaddy's 380FGB. In November, however, the whole route would be operated from South Uist by MacAulay. Highland's Ford T12 is on loan to cover a school contract to Bayhead, until the intended bus, Bedford CD77, arrives for private operator MacCuish of Sollas.

Amazingly, the MacBrayne garage in Portree is still in use today with Stagecoach, having an allocation of thirteen vehicles, although Rapson had up to twenty-three, having failed to find suitable premises elsewhere. In 1961, when there was also a depot at Ardvasar, there were ten vehicles based in Portree and six at Armadale, all small vehicles with seating capacities between twenty and twenty-nine, but only two – KGD903 and KGD909, both of which were outstationed for routes with Royal Mail contracts – had mail compartments. Bedford OLAZ KGD909 is seen emerging from the garage at Portree.

Top: Bedford OLAZ KGB261 was numerically the first of the batch of twenty-two vehicles new in 1952, of which the last twelve had mail compartments. One (KGD902) later lost it, and others had different capacities at different times. Sitting opposite the square in Portree in September 1964, it has come over from Inverness on loan to operate the Kilmaluag via Staffin service, as the regular vehicle, KGD909, is in the depot unfit. KGB261 had operated the Whitebridge–Inverness service for years, collecting the mail en route. It was withdrawn in July 1965 and ended up with Eve Construction in London.

Middle: The service from Kilmaluag to Portree via Staffin had a complicated timetable. It did not operate on a Wednesday in the winter, but in the summer there were two return journeys daily, and on a Friday it also did a couple of trips along the even more convoluted single-track road from Portree to Peinchorran. On 6 April 1965, KGD909 is at Staffin on the 5.30 p.m. return service from Portree, and returns light to Staffin, where it is parked overnight. As the next day is a Wednesday, it does not return to Portree again until departing from Kilmaluag at 12.30 on Thursday.

Bottom: Now leaving Staffin Youth Hostel heading north for Kilmaluag, KGD909 remained on this service until the autumn, being replaced by KGE243 until the definitive replacement arrived in June 1966. This was HGA981D, a Bedford VAS with a twenty-four-seat Willowbrook body and a mail compartment. It remained as the regular bus on this service until Highland took over the Skye operation, becoming CD69, and as such it continued until late 1972. Even then, the similar HGA982D and 984D took over, and it was not until 1976 that vehicles without mail compartments were allocated to this route.

Top: KGD909 passed to Invercarron of Stonehaven in December 1965, and I caught up with it again in July 1967, still in MacBrayne colours and operating a local service in Stonehaven to Brickfield, retaining its mail compartment. It later passed to Petrie of Cupar in September 1968, and to Muir's scrapyard in Kirkcaldy, which I visited regularly, but I was not to see it again. However, this model survives in preservation with KGD903 in Inverness and KGD904 in South Uist, regularly appearing at meetings, rallies, gatherings and various historical occasions.

Middle: KGD910 also had a long historical association with one route – from Kilchoan to Acharacle – and KGD908 was kept at Glenelg for the mail service to Kyle of Lochalsh. KGE242, however, had a variable seating capacity, and was effectively a spare mail bus at Fort William. When I photographed it at the Ardgour ferry in August 1962, it had twelve seats, and its large mail compartment was being filled with produce for its destination at Kilchoan, as it was deputising for KGD910, and had continued from Acharacle on to Ardgour. Withdrawn in September 1967, it was the last Bedford OLAZ in service.

Bottom: Another bus allocated to a route for years was KGB262, which sat at Kyle of Lochalsh all week, running in to Inverness on a Saturday; it left at 9.15 a.m. and arrived back at 8.50 p.m., allowing five hours in Inverness. From June to September, it also operated on Tuesdays. Replaced by Bedford VAS 377FGB in May 1962, it moved to Ardvasar, and in September 1963 I photographed it as it arrived at Broadford Crossroads on the connecting 7.30 a.m. run from Ardvasar to Kyleakin, with the screen set for 'Glasgow'. It moved to North Uist in January 1966 and on to Harris in May, joining KGE242.

The initial Highland allocation at Portree depot included full-size buses, and in October 1975 the first 36-foot-long bus, T113, a Ford R1114 with an Alexander fifty-three-seat body, arrived for the Dunvegan via Borve service. The next was T140 (NAS140R), with a Duple coach shell and bus seats, delivered in April 1977 and immediately sent to Portree to operate the Ardvasar–Kyleakin service, continuing until 1979 when it moved to Dunvegan for a school run to Portree. Here it is parked on the evening of 23 May 1977 at Ardvasar, where it remains overnight. It has still to have a destination blind fitted.

The following morning it has left at 7.55 for Kyleakin, and is returning on the 10.00 service, approaching Broadford and passing another Duple-bodied Ford T67 (UST867L), which is on the 9.30 run from Portree to Inverness. Fortunately, I managed to manoeuvre my car over a ditch to facilitate this. T67 had a complex history, and had arrived on Skye in October 1976, being used on the Ardvasar–Kyleakin service over the winter. Having a six-speed gearbox, the intention was to use it on the Inverness–Glasgow service over the summer, and it was having a trial run on this easier journey.

It did return to Skye that night, but was considered not ideal for the Glasgow service, and was transferred back to Inverness in the autumn, appearing on the Aberdeen service instead, while Leopards JL2–5 went to Glasgow. T67 was new in May 1973 as a solitary forty-nine-seat Duple-bodied Ford R1114 in coach livery, repainted red and blue before coming to Portree, and red and grey in November 1981, only to be smashed a year later and withdrawn. Here it lies broken down at Broadford on 17 April 1977, awaiting suspended tow to Inverness for a new engine.

The ubiquitous Willowbrook-bodied smaller Ford R1014 service buses fared no better on Skye, and only two were ever allocated. T74 came from Aviemore and T76 from Wick in August 1974, but both returned to their original depots in October 1977 and late 1981 respectively. Neither seemed very reliable, being parked up in school holidays, although T76 seemed to cope with the quiet service from Dunvegan via Sligachan. Here, on 26 June 1982, unusually, T65 (SST265K) from the Inverness pool has replaced T140 in the workshops there, and is parked at the driver's house at Broadford.

Top: By contrast, the Leopards proved to be popular, reliable and ideal rugged machines for coping with the poor state of many of the single-track roads on Skye at that time. The first to arrive were forty-nine-seat L21–2 (CAS515–6W) in June 1981 for the Portree–Inverness and Glasgow services. Nine months later, the first sixty-two-seaters came, L27–8 (FAS372–3X) for the Dunvegan outstation, followed by L29 (FAS374X) from Fort William in 1987. It was photographed in June on the Friday afternoon extension of the school service from Portree to Torrin on down to Elgol, now with its new fleet number, L229.

Middle: In 1990, L229 is operating the 'North End' service, which combines the former MacBrayne route, from Portree to Kilmaluag via Staffin and the east coast of the Trotternish Peninsula, with the former MacLeod route via Duntulm and the west side, later operated by Nicolson of Borve. It is near Duntulm on the anticlockwise circle. Later, in the National Express-owned division of the company, it operated for Highland Country Bus at Thurso, but when the two companies were reunited in December 1999, it ran as 155 at Portree until sold in January 2002 to Whitelaw of Stonehouse.

Bottom: The most spectacular part of the circular service was the horseshoe bend above the village of Uig. L227 is negotiating this, about to reverse before completing the manoeuvre and descending to Uig Pier, and thence on to Portree. It had a different history after Highland Scottish Omnibuses was privatised in 1991, remaining with Sandy Rapson in October 1995. It operated for Highland Bus & Coach until the formation of Rapson's Coaches, when it was numbered 153, and continued to be based in Inverness until also sold to Whitelaw in November 2001.

Top: A further two sixty-two-seat Leopards arrived from Fife in October 1983, when a decision was made to replace the D/Ds of Nicolson of Borve with S/Ds on school contracts from Kyleakin and Broadford to Portree High School. New in November 1980 as FPE152–3 at St Andrews depot, WFS152–3W became L51–2, later L251–2, kept at Broadford. L251 remained at Portree with HCB, while 252 passed to HB&C, and was renumbered 145 in Rapson's fleet. It too went to Whitelaw, in November 1980. Here it is ascending from Balmeanach, on the Friday shopper's service to Peinchorran, in June 1987.

Middle: Eight years earlier, and before Leyland Leopards had arrived on Skye, there were only five large-capacity vehicles on the island, all Fords with Alexander Y-type bodies. T113 (JST113P) was a fifty-three-seat model that arrived new, and forty-nine-seat T101–4 (HST201–4N) came when a couple of years old to replace the troublesome AEC Reliances – BA20, 25 and 29 – and the hapless Ford T67. In the event, they did not prove very reliable either, although for five years they operated the Inverness, Glasgow and Edinburgh services. Here T102 is descending to Peinchorran, after returning from repair at Inverness.

Bottom: Six months after T113 arrived, the first new coaches came to Skye when Ford R1014 models with forty-five-seat Duple Dominant bodies T117–8 (KST117–8P) were allocated for Scotia Tours. In May 1980, a further two, T166–7 (AXA301–2N), new to Fife in August 1974 as FT1–2K, arrived for tours, being delicensed during the winters. However, in April 1983, they were reallocated to Tain for new school contracts. T167, now in the red and grey bus livery, returned in September 1985 to operate the school service to Peinchorran, and has just turned round at the terminus before returning to Portree.

Five Leopards were acquired from Northern in November 1981 – NPE77–81 (GSO77–81V), becoming Highland L12–6 – although they were loaned to Fife between April and June 1982. L12–3 were later converted to sixty-two seats in December 1983, using seats obtained from Tyne and Wear. L15–6 were transferred to Fife as FPE196/5 in exchange for L51–2. L14 remained as a fifty-three-seater, moving to Highland Country Bus at Portree depot, later becoming Rapson 122. It is sitting near the driver's house by Kilmaluag in June 1992, outstationed for the 358 service to Portree via Staffin.

Having heard that there was a Highland bus sitting at Lochmaddy, I decided to pay a weekend trip in August 1971 to North Uist, sleeping in a cabin on the ferry, and on arrival was greeted by Ford Thames T12 (SSA469), one of four new to Simpson of Rosehearty in June 1960, with a Duple Yeoman body; it passed to Northern in December 1966 as NT2, and on to Highland a year later. The only one repainted in bus livery, it moved from Dingwall to Portree in April 1971 then over to North Uist in August, returning later in the year; it was withdrawn in October 1972 and sold to Hall (contractor), Aberdeen.

In the sixties, the buses of Lochs Motor Transport were kept overnight at Cameron Terrace, drivers' houses or at Crossbost itself. Parked at Crossbost on 5 November 1967 is Bedford SB3 SK6348 with a Duple Midland forty-two-seat body, new in 1958, when it was first employed at the Dounreay nuclear reactor in Caithness. It was purchased by John Mitchell of Stornoway in May 1962, passing to Lochs Motor Transport in August 1963. Parked in front is withdrawn WMP189, being cannibalised to provide parts for similar AJS451, and rear panels to SK6348 later on.

Galson Motors Bedford SB KWY559 was usually parked overnight at the depot at Lower Barvas, but sometimes, on a Thursday, it was parked near a schoolteacher's house at Ballantrushal for a school journey the following afternoon from Ness to Shader. On a Sunday, it also regularly operated a church run from Shader to Barvas. New in 1952, with the recently introduced thirty-three-seat Duple Vega body, it was acquired from Browning of Whitburn in April 1965, and replaced by Duple-bodied Ford 1306PT in January 1970.

On Monday, Tuesday and Thursday, there was a late journey from Stornoway to Galson, leaving at 9.15 p.m., and KWY559 often operated it, leaving Ness at 5.30. It is seen here crossing Barvas Moor, heading for Stornoway, on Monday 10 June 1968. Sometimes twelve-seat Morris J2BM WSM604, still in the brown and yellow livery of Carruthers of New Abbey, would take over at Barvas. On Friday and Saturday, the departure from Stornoway was at 10.15 p.m., and often thirty-six-seat Bedford SBO SJH717 would operate it.

On Wednesday 20 March 1968, KWY 559 has arrived at Barvas on the 6.15 journey from Stornoway to Ness. Parked in the foreground is SJH 717, which had been on the school service from Ness to Shader. On a Sunday it regularly operated a church run in the Ness area. New in 1954, with a Duple Super Vega body and a diesel engine, it had an oval front grille, a feature which only appeared on models built in 1954. Acquired from MacDonald of Balallan in February 1967, it had been new to Boxmoor & District of Hemel Hempstead, and was painted in to red and cream livery in 1972.

The other Bedford SB in the Galson fleet, with a thirty-three-seat Duple Vega body, was WMV418, parked in Stornoway on Tuesday 10 October 1967 for the 6.15 service to Ness. New to Williams (Corvedale Motors) of Ludlow, it was acquired from an operator in Kidderminster in May 1966, and withdrawn at the end of 1968. Parked behind is similar Bedford AJS451 of Lochs Motor Transport, acquired from Highland Omnibuses in August 1965, which is soon to leave on the 5.15 service to Ranish.

Six years later, Galson Motor Services KJS666 is arriving in Stornoway on a Saturday at 1.50 from Ness, due to depart again at 6.15. Currently kept there in a garage as a spare bus, it operates the morning school run. A Bedford SB5 with a Duple Midland forty-two-seat body, it was new with KJS555 to John Mitchell in May 1962, acquired by Galson in May 1971 to replace AST238C, and by 1979 had been withdrawn, its body ending up as a shed at Borve.

Top: Somerled Square in Portree has always been the stance for all the bus and coach departures, and, with the Portree Hotel as the backdrop, remains so to this day. This line-up was photographed in August 1971, a year after the MacBrayne operation was taken over by Highland Omnibuses. Only CD55 is in fleet livery, and beside it is HGA981D, now CD69, the regular mail bus kept at Staffin for the Kilmaluag service. Beside MacLeod's Bedford OB SX7039 are former MacBrayne VAS EGA831C, 377FGB and 382FGB, now Highland CD63 for Ardvasar, 45 on a private hire, and 47 for Kyleakin.

Middle: The route along the single-track road from Peinchorran to Portree via the Braes, which MacBrayne acquired from the Skye Transport Company in 1958, has always had a school and a Friday shoppers' service. Former MacBrayne EGA833C, now Highland CD64 on the Friday return journey, is about to join the main A87 for Portree. New to Islay in May 1965, it was transferred to Portree in July 1969, remaining until December 1972 when it joined the pool at Inverness. It was withdrawn in April 1976 and sold to the dealer Ensign of Benfleet, eventually ending up with Tally Ho of Kingsbridge.

Bottom: A year later and CD45, 47 and 64 are all in fleet livery, and parked at Ardvasar depot. Five buses were kept overnight, although there were eight officially allocated by MacBrayne at the time Highland took over. By summer 1973, only three were outstationed at the former MacBrayne garage. CD45 and 47 were new in May 1962 to Inverness for the Fort Augustus and Foyers services respectively, moving to South Uist and Ardvasar, and both passing to Highland with the Skye operation in September 1970. They were withdrawn late in 1972, and sold to Aberdeen contractors.

Top: The other route on Skye to have a bus with a mail compartment allocated was the Dunvegan–Kyleakin service via Struan and Sligachan, and when KGD909 was kept at Staffin KGD903 was at Dunvegan overnight. When it was withdrawn in spring 1965, it was replaced by Duple coach WGG629 for a year until HGA984D, with twenty-four seats and a mail compartment, finally arrived in May 1966, and continued on this service for eight years until replaced by forty-seat Bedford SB5 UGB138H, later Highland CD41. HGA984D is at Kyleakin pier on 11 July 1966, due to leave at 2.30 for Dunvegan.

Middle: By September 1974, HGA984D, now Highland CD71, is no longer required at Dunvegan, and is again sitting on the pier at Kyleakin. It is now kept at Broadford for a primary school contract from Kyleakin to Broadford, and is continuing to Armadale for a summer ferry connection back to Broadford at 5.45, connecting in turn with the bus from Kyleakin to Portree. Spending its entire life on Skye, it was withdrawn in July 1976 and sold to the dealer Ensign at Benfleet, eventually ending up on tortuous single-track roads again with Taylor & Hudson (Mountain Goat) of Windermere in 1978.

Bottom: In August 1957, the mail bus allocated to the Dunvegan service was KGE541, which joined the MacBrayne fleet in November 1958, when it took over the vehicles (all of which had mail compartments) and services of the SCWS-owned Skye Transport Company. Of the seven vehicles, two others were operated by MacBrayne: DYS933, a Duple-bodied OB, and GGA989, a SCWS-bodied Albion. Behind it is AMS342, a Bedford OWB with twenty seats and a mail compartment, ordered by Alexander to be W190, but never operated, entering service with Skye Transport in June 1945 and sold to MacLeod of Duntulm in April 1958. (Robert Grieves Collection)

Thirty-four years later, and a double-decker is operating a service run on Skye, from Kyleakin to Portree. Clan Coaches (Skyways), in addition to school and express work, operated a network of local services on Skye in the summer, competing with Highland. In July 1991, a month before Highland was privatised, Bristol VRT ANV775J is heading in service for Portree. It was purchased from United Counties Omnibus Company in 1989, having entered service as a series 2 model in July 1971 at Bedford, being one of the last flat-screen VRTs, and later converted to series 3 specification.

In school term, Clan Coaches operated a contract from Kyle of Lochalsh to Plockton High School, and was later sold to a short-lived company, Loch Lann Coaches of Culloden, based in Inverness, who used it on school work until February 2002. It was subsequently purchased for preservation and restored to its original livery. The other Skyways school contract to have a double-decker was from Ratagan to Plockton, and Park Royal-bodied Leyland Atlantean PBC11G, acquired from Leicester three years previously, is parked near the owner's house at Inverinate in June 1987, looking over Loch Duich.

Double-deckers were used on school contracts on Skye itself until the danger of operating potentially unstable vehicles on the island roads in high winds was emphasised by Dr Ball, wife of the local surgeon at Broadford, and in October 1983 these were replaced by sixty-two-seat Leyland Leopards of Highland Omnibuses. Operated by Nicolson, based at Borve, former Southdown Leyland PD3/4 FCD311D, with a Northern Counties sixty-nine-seat body, is parked at Broadford, still in NBC colours, in April 1982. Ironically, a Rapson Daimler Fleetline had to do a school run from Kyleakin to Portree one day.

Nicolson operated a mixed fleet of coaches used on contract work for businesses on the west coast, as well as school and service runs. This view, taken at the depot at Borve during the school holidays in April 1983, shows the three double-deckers. Ex-Southdown Leyland PD3 FCD311D is now in a fleet livery, and Leyland Atlantean PDR1A/1 MDW389G and PDW95H, with Alexander seventy-eight-seat bodies, have arrived from Newport. Also in the picture is a forty-one-seat Plaxton-bodied AEC Reliance, RVB412E, acquired from MacLeod of Duntulm in April 1982 but still in the livery of Clan Coaches.

Top: Sixteen years earlier, photographed at Broadford is a thirty-three-seat Duple-bodied Bedford SB, owned by A. Sutherland & Sons of Broadford, who operated tours from various points on the island and a local church run on a Sunday. In addition, it operated a weekly express service from Skye to Glasgow, introduced in 1953 under the name of 'Skye Cars', taking over from Neil Beaton of Portree, who had started the run a year earlier. In the early seventies, Wallace Arnold Tours took over the service, often using coaches from other operators. JJW696 came from Bird of St Pauls Cray in July 1963. (Robert Grieves)

Middle: The Bedford SB, with a Duple Vega thirty-three-seat body, was a common sight in the Islands, and Lochs Motor Transport acquired a couple from Highland Omnibuses in August 1965. AJS451 was new to William Ross of Balblair on the Black Isle in July 1953, for his service from Resolis to Dingwall. It was acquired by Highland Omnibuses in May 1964, given fleet number C22, converted for OMO operation, but not repainted. It continued to operate from Dingwall depot, outstationed at Resolis until delicensed in May 1965. In August 1967, it sits at its stance in Stornoway, due to depart at 5.15 for Ranish.

Bottom: In February 1968, replaced by Albion Viking BWG650B, Bedford AJS451 is sitting in the park at Leurbost as a spare bus. In the distance, on its school run from Leurbost school to Cameron Terrace, is Bedford SB SK6348, which is going to be parked up there overnight. Shortly after, eleven-seat Bedford VST554 will pass, bound for Balallan. With its Certificate of Fitness expiring at the end of December, AJS451 now only occasionally operates the school service to Cameron Terrace, and the Sunday church run.

Top: John Morrison also had a similar thirty-three-seat Bedford SB HCA177, new in June 1951 to Thomas of Eglwysbach. It had a further two owners before moving to Scotland in August 1961 to join the fleet of Hunter of Loanhead, when I travelled in it while at university in Edinburgh. It passed to King of Kirkcowan in April 1964, on to Morrison a year later, and was acquired with the business by Highland Omnibuses in June 1970. It was not operated, but ended up as a caravan on Skye. On Sunday 27 August 1967, it is parked by the roadside at Northton after its church run to Kyles Stockinish.

Middle: In March 1968, Lochs Motor Transport AJS451 is again sitting in the park at Leurbost as the spare bus. Looking away from the village is open ground, where two of the vehicles previously operated lie withdrawn, cannibalised and perhaps vandalised. Bedford SBG DSN244 was new in 1954 with a thirty-eight-seat Duple Super Vega body, an extra seat now being fitted just ahead of the entrance door. It came from Brown of Crawley in May 1959. Bedford OB KGT612 was fitted with a Mulliner thirty-seat body, and was acquired from London County Council in August 1960.

Bottom: The other Bedford SB that Lochs obtained from Highland Omnibuses was WMP189, seen here withdrawn and being cannibalised at the garage at Crossbost in April 1968. New to Fountain Luxury Coaches of Twickenham in 1952, it passed to Mayfair of Gateshead in August 1957, and to the Achnasheen Hotel Company in 1959. Highland acquired this company in March 1965, giving it fleet number C8, but it was never operated. Acquired in a brown and cream livery, it was painted in to the same red and cream livery as AJS451 before sale to Lochs, and withdrawn by July 1967.

Looking forlorn at the Lochs depot, now at Leurbost, six years later, among the withdrawn vehicles is OMS241. It is an Albion Nimbus with a twenty-nine-seat Alexander coach body, new in May 1960 to Walter Alexander in Lawson livery as N8 at Kirkintilloch depot. It was sold to Millburn Motors in February 1970, passing to Kennedy of Orinsay in March for his service to Stornoway, which ran four days a week. A year later it moved to Ross of Ardroil, who operated from Bernera to Stornoway. When I saw it at Leurbost in 1973, it had Uig Bus Service on the front, and I gather had been impounded.

Another Albion Nimbus to operate in the islands was KST52 with MacLeod Brothers at Loch Skipport, where I photographed it still in Highland livery in June 1968, parked at the end of the single-track road. It was new to Highland Omnibuses as A3 in August 1956, with an Alexander twenty-nine-seat body, and allocated to Caithness, usually at Wick depot, where it spent its entire life usually on Dounreay contract work. Sold to Macrae of Ardelve in July 1967, it was licensed by MacLeod in November of that year, and withdrawn by February 1970. Behind is eleven-seat Austin J2BA NST228, also used as a PSV.

Of the thirty-nine Bedford VAS with service bus bodies new to MacBrayne, four were sold directly to Uist operators, but, of the thirty-two that passed to Highland, only two were sold on to Lewis operators, both from the 1962 batch, which were all disposed of by 1973. 381FGB, with a thirty-seat Duple Midland body, was acquired with the Fort William operation in May 1970, numbered CD46 and moved to Dornoch. It was painted in to Highland fleet colours in March 1972, but repainted in August to red and cream for William MacDonald of Vatisker in Lewis, who licensed it in October. (Robert Grieves)

The other Bedford VAS to end up on Lewis was 386FGB, which had twenty-one seats and a mail compartment when new, and was allocated to Acharacle for the mail service to Ardgour Ferry. It remained on this route, passing to Highland in May 1970 as CD49, although this service passed to an independent, Allan MacDonald of Kinlochmoidart, a year later. It left Fort William on 28 August 1971, was painted in to fleet livery, had its mail compartment removed in September to seat twenty-eight passengers, and was reallocated to Harris. It was delicensed in October 1972, and sold to Lochs MT, with whom I eventually photographed it at Leurbost in 1974.

Top: Three of the ex-MacBrayne Bedford VAS ended up on Harris, being sold directly to the Harris Hotel Garage. Two, HGA977D and 979D, now Highland CD66 and 91, are sitting in Stornoway bus station in August 1973, due to depart at 3.30 for Tarbert and 6.00 for Northton, replacing forty-one-seat Bedford CD22 and Ford T2, both of which are unfit. CD91 was new to Islay, where it was kept at Port Charlotte, moving to the Claddach outstation in North Uist in May 1971 until MacBrayne left. It then joined the pool at Inverness, was painted in May 1972, loaned to Fort William and moved to Harris in October.

Middle: A year later and Ford Thames T3 has arrived at the bus station at 9 a.m. from Tarbert, and is due to leave at 9.30 for Rodel. New to Starks of Dunbar as T6 in April 1962, with a forty-one-seat Duple Yeoman body, it passed to Scottish Omnibuses in January 1964 as F1, becoming Highland T3 in February, at Inverness depot. It was repainted in to coach livery in April 1966, used on tours at Dingwall between 1968 and 1970, and then delicensed, apart from a loan to Skye in the summer of 1971. It moved to Harris in October 1972, where it remained until the depot closed, but did not pass to the Harris Hotel Garage.

Bottom: By 1975, two further Fords (T6 and T8 with Duple Trooper bodies) had joined T2 and T3 at Tarbert, but the Fords were notoriously unreliable, and, when only one was operational, Inverness sent over a relatively new Bedford VAM coach with a forty-one-seat Y-type Alexander body, originally purchased for the 1967 touring season. CD19 remained during July and August before returning to Inverness, and is arriving at Stornoway on the 9.30 a.m. through service from Northton. It was the only one of the batch (CD16–21) not painted in to bus livery, and was withdrawn in July 1981 and sold to Morar Motors.

Top: The bus station at Tarbert is beside the pier, and this view in August 1973 shows a typical line-up at 11.15 on a Saturday, with forty-two-seat Bedford SB JJS444 hired from Lochs Motor Transport to help out with duplication, because two of the six allocated buses are unfit. Ford T3 is still in the blue coach livery, being repainted into poppy-red and peacock-blue bus colours in May 1974, and is due to depart at 11.40 for Rodel via the 'Golden Road'. Alongside are CD91 from Northton for the 11.30 service to Stornoway, and CD66 for the 11.45 departure, with no duplicate actually being required.

Middle: A year earlier, and the vehicle line-up is very different. Bedford SB1 CD23–5 had come over from Caithness to replace three of the Bedfords acquired with the operation of Morrison in June 1970, only FYJ847 (CD78) remaining until replaced by CD22 in June 1971. They remained until October 1972, to be replaced by Fords T2–4, but T4 never came, CD66 arriving instead. CD25 is for Rodel, CD22 the 11.45 to Stornoway, CD23 (the only one to get bus livery) the 11.30, and Lochs LJS500J is on a hire. The Mclennan midi is for Husinish, and the blue microbus MJS367J hired for Kyles mail.

Bottom: On returning to Inverness, CD23–5 (SSA472–4) were painted before sale to Peace of Kirkwall, and 24 and 25 are parked ready to leave in April 1973 for a further four years' service. The trio had been new to Simpson of Rosehearty in July 1960, acquired by Alexander (Northern) in December 1966 as NW266–8, before moving to Highland a year later. Lined up beside them are Albion Viking AV7 (FGM105D) in for repair, AEC Reliance B34 (RST454) from Thurso down to be repainted into bus livery, and 1972-accident-victim B22 (MST805) from Wick, destined for Kelbie (dealer) at Turriff later in the year.

Top: Bedford CD22 (WAW355) was unique in the Highland fleet with its Burlingham Seagull 61 body. It was new to Whittle of Highley as No. 17 in February 1961, but withdrawn a year later, next appearing with Miller of Calderbank in 1963, and passing to Seaforth MacGregor of Dornoch in May 1964. Highland took over his small operation three years later, with Duple-bodied Albion FT39AL LVD635, acquired from Hebridean Transport, and eleven-seat Kenex-bodied Austin J2VA NS3922. CD22 has just arrived at Inverness in May 1967 for attention, but would return to Dornoch, still in MacGregor's livery.

Middle: It was 'unwanted' at Dornoch, and used little, leaving in June 1970. Now in the blue coach livery, it was transferred to Skye soon after the MacBrayne operation was taken over in September 1970. It crossed over to Harris in June 1971, remaining there to be taken over by the Harris Garage in December 1975, when it was used for spares. Here it sits in the bus park at Tarbert, due to leave at 11.45 for Stornoway. Bedford CD25, kept at Northton, has operated the 9.30 service from Rodel via Borve, and is waiting to return at 11.40, while CD23 is coming light from Northton to duplicate CD22.

Bottom: CD22 was painted into the peacock-blue and poppy-red service bus livery in March 1973, but was back in Inverness a year later for a body overhaul, and is sitting in Portree depot in July 1974 unfit, on its way back to Harris. Also receiving attention is HGA982D, new with twenty-four seats and a mail compartment for the Glenelg–Kyle route. Now CD70, this has been replaced with four more seats. Moved to Dornoch in late 1975, it returned to Skye in March 1978 with MacLeod at Dunvegan. Beside it is twenty-nine-seat EGA829C, now CD61, a spare bus, unfit since February and still so in September.

Top: By September 1974, CD22 is back on Harris, and is parked up at the bus stance off the school service to Kyles of Scalpay. Replacement Bedford CD15 (MSO579), with a Duple Bella Vega body, is still here, and is at Northton for the afternoon Stockinish school run, as six operational buses are required today. CD66 is ready for the 11.40 service to Rodel, Ford Thames T2 (FSS929) from Northton for the 11.30 to Stornoway, and T3 (430YTD) the 11.45 service. CD91 is at the depot for the Maruig school run, with T6 laid up there, while T8 has still to make it over from Skye. T2, like T3, was new to Starks.

Middle: A year earlier, and CD22 lies at the depot at Tarbert unfit. Highland Omnibuses continued to use the depot premises that MacBrayne took over from the Harris Hotel Garage until it was sold back in December 1975. Also parked there in the evening are T3 in from Northton, sitting on the pit; CD50 off the Kyles of Scalpay run; and in the foreground CD66 (HGA977D), which has arrived from Stornoway. It was new to Ardvasar in May 1966, crossing to Harris in May 1973. Like CD91, it passed to the Harris Garage, and was not withdrawn until 1983, ending up as a garden shed on Lewis.

Bottom: CD91, on the other hand, was sold on locally to Morrison of West Tarbert in August 1978, ending up as a shed nearby. A third Bedford VAS was acquired by Harris Garage: EGA826C, new in May 1965 to Kinlochleven for the Ballachulish service, later at Oban, becoming Highland CD58 in May 1970. Moving to Fort William, it reached Harris in October 1975, and four years later on to Lewis, running for Kennedy of Orinsay, ending up as a peat store at Bragar. Although CD22 is parked up at Tarbert, T2 is also unfit, lying at the former Morrison depot at Northton, where CD91 is parked overnight, too.

Top: Only one of the vehicles in the original Harris Hotel fleet was operated: eleven-seat Kenex-bodied Ford NST683, new in June 1959 and used on the Friday service to Maruig. It was intended to move it to Glenelg for the run to Kyle during winter 1967, but it remained on Harris until withdrawn on 30 January 1968. For many years I had visited Mr 'JR' Cameron, the General Manager of MacBrayne, at his office at Lancefield Street, Glasgow, for information about the movements of the buses. When he was up in Stornoway, he offered it to me, but as I had nowhere to keep it at that time it was sold for scrap.

Middle: Malcolm McLennan of Govic also operated a service on North Harris on a Tuesday and a Saturday, from Tarbert west to Husinish, and the mail ferry to Scarp, along the north shore of West Loch Tarbert. Acquired in October 1970 from Edwards of Liverpool, LTD795C is a Bedford J2SZ10 with a Duple Midland nineteen-seat body. Interestingly, it replaced a Ford, 326RKO, similar to MacBrayne's NST683, which had just been relicensed again. It is parked at the bus stance at Tarbert in August 1972, due to depart at 2.30.

Bottom: The previous vehicle to operate the service was ex-MacBrayne Bedford OLAZ KGB268, acquired in June 1966 directly from their garage at Tarbert, entering service in August. New in September 1952, with a twenty-five-seat Duple Sportsman body, it and KGB267 had later been fitted with roof windows. It was transferred from North Uist to Harris at the time of the takeover. Photographed just outside Tarbert in September 1967, having brought in Communion attenders, it was derelict by 1970. Its body was later sold to a local farmer for a bothy, and the chassis dumped in a lochan with wheels still visible.

Top: Operators in the more remote areas of the Highlands had a long history of using small, unusual buses, often purpose-built for rural services, or acquired second-hand for a specific route. John Morrison operated a Bedford A3LZ, with a twenty-one-seat Spurling body, not dissimilar to the one operated by John Bain of North Erradale on his Gairloch–Melvaig service, but without a mail compartment. New in 1955 to Thirlwell of Gateshead, it was acquired from RH Robson of Hexham in September 1963. It was photographed out of use at the garage in August 1967, and withdrawn a year later.

Middle: Also showing the signs of its previous owner, but displayed on the boot rather than in the destination box, is MSN195, a thirteen-seat Trojan new to McTavish of Arrochar in May 1966. It was sold to the Stag Garage at Lochgilphead seven months later, and has just arrived at Carloway, where Donald Morrison is going to use it on a service to Shawbost school. It was photographed on 14 September 1967.

Bottom: An unusual small bus that ran on Islay was SB7743, a Bedford MLZ in the fleet of Harry Caskie, who owned shops in Bowmore as well as running a bus company. It was one of two eighteen-seat coaches new to Gold Line of Dunoon in December 1949, with very rare bodies constructed by Binnie of Wishaw, a specialist bodybuilder with a variety of products. Now with nineteen seats, it is leaving Port Ellen at 8.10 a.m. on its school run from Ardbeg to Bowmore in 1965. Caskie's buses could also be seen on the pier at Port Ellen when the boat came in with supplies for the shops. It was withdrawn a year later.

Top: Another private operator on Islay was J. A. Bell of Ballygrant, the longest-established village on Islay. Tours were operated from Ballygrant, and a Thursday service via Bridgend to Bowmore. Parked in the yard at the garage in May 1965 is FSB211, a Bedford SB with a forty-one-seat Duple Super Vega body, new in 1960 to Gold Line of Dunoon. Still carrying their fleet name on the side, it was acquired in April 1965. The other vehicle he operated was a Bedford OB JSM272, acquired from Whiteford of Shotts.

Middle: There were few coaches with full-size Burlingham Seagull bodies operated in the Western Isles. Sutherland of Glenbrittle routinely obtained his vehicles from Highland, painted in to this livery in Inverness, and usually one every year. In Portree square, in September 1968, is Bedford SBO RVM34 with a thirty-six-seat body, new to Makinson of Manchester in 1955, passing later to Smith of Grantown in December 1961. Taken over by Highland in December 1966 as CD14, it was withdrawn in April 1968, moved to Skye in August, withdrawn in late 1971, returned to Highland and sold to the dealer Kelbie.

Bottom: Morrison of Northton had a mixed fleet of Bedfords, and EMS829 also had a Seagull body. New in June 1953 to Alexander as W246, a thirty-one-seat coach for extended tours, it was latterly used at the Callander sub-depot of Stirling. It came to Harris in October 1966 via the dealer Millburn Motors, passing to Highland in June 1970, but was not operated, and ended up as a caravan on Benbecula. It is parked at Scott Road, Tarbert, in June 1968 off its regular school run from Stockinish to Leverburgh. Apart from a Sunday church run it did little else, as it proved not very economical.

Top: Donald Smith of Carnish operated a service from Brenish to Stornoway via Garynahine on Monday, Tuesday, Thursday and Friday. GJS586 is seen here on a Saturday private hire, arriving at Tarbert pier in August 1972, still in the livery of its previous owner, Gibson of Moffat, from whom it had been acquired nine months previously. A Ford Thames 570E with a Duple Yeoman forty-one-seat body, it was sold a few months later to the dealer S&N of Bishopbriggs, and ended up as a car transporter.

Middle: Dodson of Stornoway acquired an unusual Bedford J4LZ2 with a twenty-nine-seat Plaxton Embassy body from Conroy of Belfast in May 1973, and used it on an official tour. Photographed here in Stornoway bus park in August 1975, it was withdrawn by 1980. It is interesting to speculate how the face of public transport might have been altered if MacBrayne had succeeded in purchasing the business of John Mitchell back in 1963: whether Highland Omnibuses would have subsequently developed this operation as they did on Skye, and if there would today be a 'Stagecoach in the Western Isles'.

Bottom: Also on a tour, about to leave from the MacBrayne terminal by the pier, is Hebridean Transport's GJS418N, a Bedford SB5 with a Duple Dominant body. Despite the body shell, it has forty-one bus-style seats and is usually kept at Upper Bayble with the fleet engineer. Although effectively a spare bus, it was primarily used for tours. Photographed in August 1975, it was six months old, having replaced JJS628, which had been sold to Lochs Motor Transport.

The first MacBrayne vehicle to be based in Lewis and Harris was a Bedford C5 with a Duple twenty-nine-seat coach body: 605CYS, new in May 1961 and immediately sent north to provide local tours for tourists arriving on the *Loch Seaforth* at Stornoway and the *Lochmor* at Tarbert. A year later it was replaced by newly arrived Bedford VAS 375FGB. With the introduction of the car ferries in 1964, the vehicles on the extended tours now came on to the islands, and 373FGB is seen here in Stornoway with Lews Castle in the background. It was sold as early as 1968 to SMT (as dealer), later to Wright of Nenthead.

A total of twenty-four Bedford VAS with Duple Bella Vista bodies were purchased between 1962 and 1969. Of the first batch of eight, two others were sold to SMT, three passed to Highland as their CD42–4, and two to Midland. All the remainder joined the Midland fleet. The four oldest were never operated by Midland, but the remainder became MW295–308. OYS111F is on an extended tour in Benbecula, near Balivanich, in July 1968 when only two months old. In October 1970, it became Midland MW303 at Milngavie depot, where I sometimes travelled on it, operating peak-time runs on our local route.

The last eleven Duple bodies were to the Vista 25 design, with a later grille design, which appears on HGA987D, seen here at Ardvasar in July 1966 when new. It became MW298 at Stepps depot, but was soon sold in November 1971, when only five years old, to SMT Sales & Service, and I haven't traced it since. EGE318C, a year older, became MW297 at Stepps, and also went to SMT, passing to Fendrick & Parsons at Littleport. Midland sadly found little use for these coaches, although HGA988D later became Alexander (Northern) NW201 at Dundee depot for an airport service.

The third member of the 1966 trio of coaches (MacBrayne fleet numbers 213–5) was HYS198D, which was exhibited at the SMT Motor Show in Glasgow in November 1965, and entered service in May 1966. As 213 it should have been registered HGA986D. Becoming MW300 at Balfron depot, it was allocated for an extended tour in summer 1971, but also sold to SMT in November that year, passing to Bentley of Bradford. Photographed at Ardvasar depot in July 1968, it is parked beside DRS886, a 7-ton Albion lorry new in 1950, acquired from Steele of Carbost in October 1963 and sold in December 1968.

MacBrayne also required larger coaches, and after ten years purchased the Bedford SB model again, but this time with forty-one-seat Plaxton bodies. Twelve arrived between 1967 and 1970, with only one in each of the last two years. One passed to Highland with the Inverness operation and one from Skye, becoming CD39–40 in 1970. The remainder, narrower at only 7 feet 6 inches wide, were on Mull, and became CD80–8/90 in November 1971. PGD216F, from the 1968 batch, is parked on the pier at Armadale in July when only two months old, and remained on Skye for its entire life, becoming Highland CD40.

In April 1972, CD40 was painted in to the Highland two-tone blue coach livery, and is again parked at Ardvasar, this time at the depot in August 1973. Parked beside it is AEC Reliance B40 (SST996), transferred from Dornoch to Skye when Highland took over, and now operates the weekly service to Edinburgh jointly with Eastern Scottish. New in May 1962 with a thirty-eight-seat Alexander body in maroon and cream, it was painted in to coach colours in May 1971 and bus livery in February 1973. Moved to Wick in 1975 for Dounreay contracts, it was sold to MacAulay of Lochboisdale in June 1977.

While initially used as a coach for island tours and private hire, CD40 was soon used as a service bus. Meanwhile, PGD215F (CD39), which had gone to Inverness when taken in to the Highland fleet, had arrived on Skye in 1976 after a few months in Fort William, and both vehicles remained on the island until withdrawn in September 1979. From 1976 to 1978, CD40 was the regular bus on the Portree–Kilmaluag via Staffin service, and is ready to leave Portree depot on 18 September 1976 for the 11.35 departure. Inside, but barely visible, is the common sight of an unfit AEC Reliance, BA29 (EWS118D).

CD39 was still stored for the winter on 28 March 1978, when I photographed CD40 near Floddigarry on the 4.10 service from Portree. Interestingly, I noted that the regular driver was off that week, and the service was operated from Portree itself. Two months later, it was painted in the later coach livery with a blue roof. The following winter it was CD40 that was delicensed, and CD39 operated the Kilmaluag service. Both were sold to Peace of Kirkwall in Orkney in January 1980, with CD39 later passing to Allan of Birsay, and on to Shalder Coaches. CD40 ended up in a garden centre near Nairn.

The remainder of the Plaxton coaches were allocated to Mull, and when Highland withdrew in April 1976 only CD83 (MGB287E) had left the island, after moving to Thurso from winter storage at Oban. CD87 is parked at the garage at Tobermory in October 1973 beside CD93, having been painted in to blue coach livery in March 1972. It was transferred to Inverness on closure, fitted for OMO operation the following year, and in 1978 moved to Nairn for tours and service work, being withdrawn in May 1980. Sold to Peace of Kirkwall in November, it later ended up parked beside CD40.

With its fullest complement of licensed vehicles, Mull had two service buses and a Bedford VAS with a Duple Bella Vista body, CD44 (376FGB), in addition to the nine Plaxton coaches. Lined up beside it near Craignure Pier in August 1974 are CD87 (PGD220F), FCD84 (PGD217F) and CD81 (MGB285E). When the Mull operation closed, they were transferred to Oban, Inverness, Aviemore and Dingwall respectively. The three larger coaches were infrequently used, and on a variety of duties; they were all withdrawn in 1980, being sold to Peace. CD44 was sold early in 1977 to MacDonald of Acharacle.

The smaller service bus was CD93 (HGA983D), a Bedford VAS with a twenty-four-seat Willowbrook body and mail compartment, new to MacBrayne in May 1966 and allocated to Islay for the inter-ferry service, replacing YYS174. Transferred to Highland ownership in January 1972, it was painted in to fleet livery in May, and left Islay for Mull in September, remaining for two years. It then went to Thurso as a spare mail bus for the Tongue service, and as a tow wagon, latterly used as an NPSV, being withdrawn in 1978. It is sitting on Craignure Pier for its regular mail run at 7.10 a.m. to Tobermory in October 1973.

With this service incorporating a double run down to the pier at Fishnish since April, CD93 is returning along what is effectively a forest track through the woods, to join the main road on its journey north, a total of 21 miles from Craignure to Tobermory. Connecting with the *Columba*, which has sailed from Oban to Craignure, it is bringing mail and goods from the mainland. Although withdrawn in January, it was October before it was sold to the Northern Constabulary in Inverness, later with Strathtay as S1 for a Forfar school contract, and is now preserved at the Glasgow Vintage Vehicle Trust Museum at Bridgeton.

Top: There were only five of the Bedford SBG (petrol engine) models bought new by MacBrayne before those with Plaxton bodies, and they arrived in two batches. In May 1955, OGB467–9 were delivered with thirty-six-seat Duple bodies to the Super Vega design introduced in 1952, and with the butterfly grille introduced in 1955. They were all withdrawn in 1968, but OGB467 and 469 were modified in Glasgow, appearing in May 1964 with an extended boot, reducing the seating capacity to thirty-one. OGB467 is sitting on the pier at Craignure in September 1964, due to depart at 1.00 for Tobermory.

Middle: This conversion was carried out because the three car ferries introduced in 1964 increased the number of passengers arriving on both Mull and Skye. The *Clansman*, arriving at Armadale from Mallaig on the mainland, generated cross-island traffic bound for Uig and on to the *Hebrides*, which sailed from Skye to Lochmaddy on North Uist, and Tarbert on Harris. OGB469 was photographed in the same month, arriving in Portree on the connecting service from Uig to Armadale. Having originally been based at Fort William, it, however, went to Glasgow for the winter.

Bottom: Having left Uig pier at 8.50 a.m., OGB469 has finally arrived at Armadale Pier at 11.35 and is now loading for its return journey at 2.30 to Portree, arriving back at Armadale at 7.35 p.m. The Portree–Kyleakin service was operated by Bedford C5 models, both bus and coach, mainly from the 1959 intake, and later Bedford VAS. The C5 models with Duple Midland twenty-eight-seat bodies were particularly suitable as they had simple driver-operated passenger doors and smaller wheels, resulting in a lower chassis with fewer steps. Unusually they had one less seat than the coaches.

Top: However, the third member of that batch, OGB468, remained in Inverness, retaining its black rear wing, and is sitting in the depot off-licence. Having previously operated the Inverness–Fort William service, it was used on tours and private hires until it moved down to Fort William in 1964 to replace OGB469. Based there, it was on loan to Skye during the summer of 1966, and was delicensed during the winters at Kinlochleven. In 1968 it did not return to service until May, when it was sent to Tobermory for a couple of months. It was sold to the contractor Rankin in Dunoon in October.

Middle: It was OGB467 that returned from winter storage at Glasgow to Skye in May for the 1965 season, while OGB469 arrived on Mull in March 1965, and remained there until withdrawn in June 1968, passing to Roger of Longside, near Peterhead, in September. From 1961 there was a policy to repaint the cream area below the windows red on Duple Super Vega and Super Vista bodies, and in 1965 both OGB467 and 469 were so treated. By July 1966, the Floddigarry north end tour required a larger bus, and OGB467 was reallocated to this duty, and is seen here at Portree Square.

Bottom: This view shows the arrangement whereby the rear seats have been removed to allow additional luggage space. OGB467 remained on Skye, being delicensed from autumn 1967. It was stored at Uig in the summer of 1968, finally moving to Glasgow in February 1969. However, it was not sold until September 1970, when it went down to the dealer Telefilms in Preston, before passing to Five Star Cleaners in Chester as a staff bus, where it remained until May 1973. No new buses were purchased by MacBrayne in 1956, and it was not until March 1957 that the other two Bedford SBGs arrived.

MacBrayne acquired an additional Bedford with a thirty-six-seat Duple Super Vega body when it took over the business of Cowe of Tobermory in May 1964. However, ASB437 was an SBO model with a Perkins diesel engine, and had an oval grille, a feature only available for the 1954 season. It was, however, new to Gold Line Motors of Dunoon in April 1955, passing to Cowe by June 1960. Painted in to fleet livery with red below the windows, it was converted to thirty seats with an extended boot, and was allocated to Ardvasar depot on Skye, where it is sitting in September 1964 beside OLAZ KGB262.

It was transferred back to Mull in July 1965, where it remained until delicensed in 1968. It then moved to a third island when it was sold to Caskie of Bowmore on Islay in September, but was withdrawn two years later. Three Bedfords from Cowe's fleet were painted in to fleet livery, and operated until 1968, or 1970 in the case of the C5Z ESY 89; they all ended up on different islands. However, three OBs with Duple Vista bodies – SB7264, EF9219 and KVO975 – were also acquired, but removed to storage in Glasgow where they remained for some time before being disposed of.

The 'steamer' service on Skye required two buses, which alternated night about between the depots at Portree and Ardvasar, although of course there was no service on a Sunday. OGB467 is sitting by the pier at Armadale, later to return on the 5.10 connection to Uig, arriving back at Portree for the night at 8.45 p.m. The destination screen is above the front bumper, unlike on the later pair, where it is incorporated in to the bumper and at risk of being sprayed by passing vehicles. The butterfly grille was specified, as for the Maudslay and AEC chassis, which were re-bodied by Duple.

The other bus on the daily changeover was SGE427, one of the two forty-one-seat Bedford SBGs, new in March 1957, seen here parked at Ardvasar depot in August 1967. It was transferred from Fort William to replace ASB437, being transferred on paper to Portree in May 1968. It was still operating this service when I saw it on 30 September 1968, but moved to Glasgow in March 1969 for disposal. The other Bedford delivered that year, SGE428, moved from Fort William to Tobermory in September 1966, remaining until replaced by a Bedford SB5 with a forty-seat Willowbrook body in September 1969.

SGE427 was also used on private hires and tours, being the first and only MacBrayne vehicle on Skye with a seating capacity of forty-one for the three years until PGD216F arrived in May 1968. It is parked here on the pier at Kyleakin beside WGG630 in September 1965. SGE427 was sold soon after arriving in Glasgow, passing to Grant of Fort Augustus two months later for a school contract. A year later it was acquired by Smith of Easdale for the Oban service, moving north to Benderloch in May 1972 where MacColl ran it for three years. SGE428 was sold to the contractor Rankin in Dunoon.

Only one out of a total of twenty-seven Bedfords with C5 chassis acquired by Highland Omnibuses was painted in to fleet colours. This happened to be numerically the first: WGG545, new in May 1959, which became C20 when acquired with the Harris operation in June 1971. It was immediately painted in to coach livery, and fortunately I went up to Tarbert to photograph it in September, as it was withdrawn the following month. In February 1972 it was sold to Ramsay of Elsrickle near Carnwath, and I often drove past it looking smart in its canary-yellow livery. It was acquired by Wilson of Stonehouse in 1976.

The second Bedford C5, with a mail compartment and Duple coach body, was 610CYS, new in June 1961, allocated to Islay where it joined YYS174. It spent its entire life on the island, passing to Highland in January 1972 as C29, and replaced in March by Bedford VAS EGA832C, now CD79 from Mull. Sold to Dundee Hospital Board, it later became a mobile caravan. Although a spare bus for YYS174 on the inter-ferry service, it was kept at the depot at Port Ellen for shoppers' services from Ardbeg, and connections with the BEA flights between Glasgow and the airport at Glenegedale.

An interesting Bedford with a Duple Super Vista body to run on Skye was NS3924, which was new to Seaforth MacGregor of Dornoch in July 1959. NS3922–3 were eleven-seat Austins also purchased that year, and NS3922 was acquired by Highland Omnibuses in May 1967, becoming MB5. NS3924, however, was sold earlier, in March 1965, to Clan Garage (later Skyways) of Kyle of Lochalsh, who operated it for nine years. It remains in MacGregor's livery eighteen months later. A Bedford C4Z2, it was based on a lorry chassis, modified to a 4-ton forward-control model with a petrol engine.

The mainstay of the MacBrayne services on Skye from 1959 for the next few years was the batch of Bedford C5 buses and coaches. Of the seven with twenty-eight-seat Duple Midland bus bodies, WGG622/5–7 ran on Skye, WGG621 was at Inverness, WGG623 at Ballachulish, and 624 at Fort Augustus. Of the first batch of coaches, WGG545/629–31 were on Skye, 632 at Fort William, and 633 at Whitebridge, although there were some exchanges between Fort William and Skye. In later years, they all tended to migrate out to Uist and Harris. Here, two of the bus bodied vehicles sit on the pier at Kyleakin. (Robert Grieves)

WGG627 was originally based at Armadale, although occasionally outstationed at Kyle of Lochalsh for the Inverness service. It remained on Skye for its entire life and passed to Highland with the Skye operation in September 1970, becoming C5, and was sold in April 1971 to Alexander Hall (builders), Aberdeen. Here it is operating the 8 a.m. departure from Ardvasar to Kyleakin, which was essentially a mail run and did not reach the ferry until 9.30. Photographed at Broadford Crossroads in September 1963, it did not go in to the village.

Sitting on the pier at Armadale is WGG627, which has arrived from Kyleakin at 11.5, calling in at Broadford Post Office on the way back. Parked beside it are WGG630–1; 609CYS, a 1961 Bedford C5 on tour; and 382FGB, a 1962 Bedford VAS which has arrived from Portree at 11.00. While WGG630 remained at Ardvasar until January 1968 when it moved to Harris, WGG631 stayed on Skye, originally allocated to Ardvasar, but later appearing on the Portree allocation list. As Highland C6, it was sold to the dealer S&N of Bishopbriggs, and returned to Skye, running for MacKinnon of Elgol.

Parked at the depot at Ardvasar, just along from Armadale Pier, that evening are the same five buses with another Bedford VAS, 379FGB, and GUS630, a 4-ton Thornycroft tipper lorry, fleet number L104, new in 1949 and sold in 1966. 379FGB and 382FGB are allocated to Ardvasar, the former from new and the latter relocated from Foyers. 609CYS came from Fort William in June 1963. It and 382 FGB remained at Ardvasar until absorbed in to the Highland fleet, becoming C18 and CD47. Having a petrol engine, like the remainder of the C class, C18 was rapidly disposed of and sold to Northern Roadways in February 1963.

Top: WGG623 had an interesting
life, moving on to its fourth
owner when sixteen years old.
Sitting here outside the garage at
Lochmaddy in June 1968, it has
been on loan from Ardvasar since
January to provide a spare bus
for the Clachan school run, and
Tuesday and Thursday tours, and
will return next month. However,
from January 1969, the North Uist
allocation was reduced to four
buses with no spare vehicle, and the
three buses on South Uist were all
required on school days. WGG623
was delicensed during the winter at
Ardvasar, and passed to Highland
in September 1970, becoming C2.

Middle: Highland Omnibuses sold
it to Carruthers of New Abbey,
fleet number 10, in April 1971, and
I photographed it at Kirkbean in
July 1974. A year later, it passed to
the contractor Whatlings, based
in Glasgow, and I caught up with
it again in May 1976 when I came
across it parked on a construction
site near Tomatin, with the
destination 'Croy Tours!' How
long it remained with them I don't
know, but of the seven bus bodied
Bedford C5 vehicles, all had been
sold by April 1971, apart from one
on Harris, WGG622. Interestingly,
only it and another based there,
WGG625, continued to operate on
the islands.

Bottom: WGG623 certainly had
a nomadic life, starting off at
Kinlochleven depot when new in
May 1959, and garaged at South
Ballachulish for the service from
the ferry to Kinlochleven. It
was then briefly outstationed at
Lochgoilhead in 1965 to operate the
run from Carrick Castle to the 'Top
of the Rest and Be Thankful', before
reaching Oban in May 1965. The
following month it went further
west to Mull, where it stayed for
two years before reaching Ardvasar
in June 1967. Such a progression of a
bus to more remote rural depots as
it aged was the norm for small buses
in the MacBrayne fleet.

Top: Another bus to be cascaded out to the periphery of the MacBrayne empire was WGG622, allocated to Portree depot, seen here parked outside the small garage at Kyleakin in September 1963. It later took up the 4.45 return trip from Kyleakin ferry to Portree, where it arrived at 6.15 and was garaged for the night. After seven years on Skye, it left for North Uist in September 1966, and on to Harris in March 1971, becoming Highland C19 in June. It remained until November, when it returned to North Uist, which was still controlled by MacBrayne, who transferred the licenses to MacLean of Grimsay.

Middle: This occurred on 29 January 1972, but the actual operation changed in November 1971. Maclean, previously a haulage contractor, took over the Lochmaddy–Baleloch Circle, but the Grenitote–Lochmaddy service was cancelled. WGG622 later passed to Garbutt of Gramsdale in December 1973, and was eventually stripped for spares. I photographed it in June 1968, while outstationed at Grenitote for the service to Lochmaddy via Newton Ferry, which included a MWF 10 p.m. ferry connection at Lochmaddy. It also operated a school run from Newton Ferry to Sollas and Bayhead.

Bottom: While at Tarbert depot, I photographed it in August 1971 beside CD24. Having had continuing access to depot allocations and movements, vehicle schedules, repaint dates and other information about the vehicles of Highland Omnibuses for many years, coupled with equivalent information (other than repaint dates) about the MacBrayne fleet, it has been possible to build up a picture of the activity around the break-up of the MacBrayne empire. There are, however, many missing pieces to the jigsaw – such as Highland CD76, operating from Western's Ardrishaig depot in MacBrayne livery; C19, above, returning to MacBrayne ownership at Lochmaddy; and C4 (WGG626) at Inverness loaned back to MacBrayne at Ardvasar in May 1970, to cover for WGG621 at Highland's workshop at Inverness.

Parked inside the Harris Hotel Garage in Tarbert on a dreich July day in 1966 are Bedford OLAZ KGB262 and KGE242. Sadly, my slide with sheep milling around them was one which was never returned. The original two buses sent over to Harris in February 1964 for the school contracts were KGE242 and KGB268. The latter was replaced in May 1966 by KGB262, when it moved west to Mclennan at Govic. KGE242 had been a spare mail bus at Fort William, now with twenty seats. It was replaced by WGG625 in April 1967, moving to Uig on Skye as a parcel bus, and sold to Garron of Strathmiglo in September.

Two years later, these two Bedfords have gone, replaced by C5 models coach WGG630 and service bus WGG625. The latter had been on Skye since new, and was used on Harris for Communion runs and the Maruig school service. It was transferred on paper to Highland in June 1971 with the Tarbert operation, and may have been numbered C22, but left the island in March when WGG622 arrived on loan from North Uist. WGG625 was then sold to Sutherland of Glenbrittle on Skye. Also parked at the depot for the Sunday is Bedford Bella Vista 373FGB, up on an extended tour.

Six years later and the petrol engine Bedford C5s have been replaced by Bedford VAS models, and 845HUS, now Highland CD50, is parked at the depot off the Kyles of Scalpay run beside Ford T3. A month later, in August, it passed to Central SMT as CS5 for East Kilbride local services, being sold to Tiger of Salsburgh in March 1977. It first entered service with MacBrayne from Inverness in June 1963 on the Foyers service. After passing to Highland in April 1970, it moved to Fort William, arriving on Harris in October 1971 to replace WGG622, on loan from North Uist.

Two years earlier, it is sitting at the former depot of John Morrison at Northton in South Harris. Painted in to fleet livery before transfer, it was the first Highland bus to operate in red and blue colours on Harris. Parked beside it is CD25, but there are also still withdrawn vehicles from the Morrison fleet that had not passed to Highland in June 1970: Bedfords GDK852 and ECN652. Highland continued to outstation buses at Northton until selling their Harris operation in December 1975 to David Cameron, son of Tom, who had sold the company to MacBrayne eleven years earlier. (Robert Grieves)

Top: After Highland sold its Mull operation in April 1976, Skye was the only island from the MacBrayne empire on which it continued to operate. AEC Reliance LUS 524E, new in June 1967 for the Glasgow–Campbeltown service, received coach livery in April 1972, and was transferred to Portree in May 1973 for the weekly Uig–Edinburgh service. Now BA20, it has stopped at Kyleakin on the return journey from Glasgow to Uig on 4 July 1974. Three years later, it was transferred to Thurso for Dounreay contracts and delicensed in July 1981. Now preserved, it appears at events all over the UK.

Middle: The other AEC with a forty-nine-seat Willowbrook body, PGE429F, entered service a year later on the Campbeltown run, displacing LUS524E to Fort William. Becoming Highland BA25 in October 1970, it moved to Skye in May 1974. Sitting at Broadford at 1.00 on 28 July 1975, despite its manual door, it is operating a local service from Portree to Kyleakin. In front is Eastern Scottish Bristol RELH6G ZA187A, bound for Ardvasar. Converted from a London toilet coach, it now has forty-nine seats, but with a power-operated door. Up on the weekly Edinburgh service, it has been hijacked for local work on Skye.

Bottom: BA25 has now returned to Portree, and is sitting in Somerled Square behind Midland Leyland Leopard MPE150Ss, which has arrived from Glasgow on the daily changeover, today with MPE32Ss, as Highland Ford T76 is unfit at Stepps depot. The summertime Monday service to Edinburgh is operated by Eastern Scottish ZA186 and 175, as Highland BA29 (EWS118D), a former Eastern Scottish Reliance, is unfit in Edinburgh (and BA20 likewise at Fort William). Also in the square is Willowbrook-bodied Bedford VAM70 CD38, the duplicate from Kyleakin, and Bedford NS3924, now in Clan Garage colours.

Top: Highland acquired identical former London coaches from Western Scottish, DSD701–2D (MT2060–1), in June 1971, numbered SL2–3. The latter had the toilet removed, and forty-nine dual-purpose seats fitted in September 1972, but returned to Western in July 1978. On Monday 30 September 1974, it is passing Uig YH on the 8.45 a.m. service from Uig to Glasgow, changing over with Midland MPE150Ss. An Inverness bus, it had in fact arrived at Portree from Edinburgh on the Saturday due to a complicated series of changeovers, as both BA20 and 25 were unfit at Inverness, and T76 again, at Fort William.

Middle: Leyland Leopards proved more reliable for the long-distance services, and this colourful scene at Portree on Saturday 27 June 1981 shows the morning departures lined up. Eastern Scottish Seddon ZS915F from Linlithgow depot, the regular Eastern Scottish coach on the Edinburgh service, has sat in Portree garage all week, and would change over with Highland T103 (HST203N), a none-too-reliable forty-nine-seat Alexander-bodied Ford R1114, which would certainly have been used by Eastern Scottish. Highland Leopard L21 (CAS515W) is ready to leave on its daily 9.30 service to Inverness and back.

Bottom: Now on the ferry, and soon to leave Kyleakin for Kyle of Lochalsh and the A87, Midland MPE267Ss (GLS267S), a 1978 Leyland Leopard with a forty-nine-seat Alexander T-type body (later Kelvin Scottish E267D, becoming 2006), takes up the rear. It is heading south for Glasgow on its regular schedule, to change over with Portree's other newly arrived Leyland Leopard L22 (CAS516W). Unusually, no duplicate has been required so far, although Ford T104 was standing by at Portree, and L23 will be at Fort William. Inverness-based Leopard L20 will pass the convoy at Inverinate en route from Inverness to Portree.

Top: Passing Lochs Motor
Transport Bedford SK6348, parked
at Cameron Terrace after its school
contract from Leurbost primary
school, is Dodge demonstrator
3033PE, now with Alexander
MacDonald of Balallan. It is on
its regular school service from the
Nicolson Institute through Balallan
to the county boundary, whence it
would return to Balallan, where it
is parked overnight. Sometimes if a
Lochs Motor Transport vehicle was
on a private hire or not available,
it would run in to Stornoway to
operate the 5.15 service to Ranish,
and on a Sunday it would be used
on a church run from Laxy.

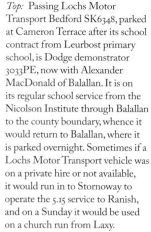

Middle: Bedford SK6348 was 7 feet
6 inches wide, and was the principal
vehicle used on the Stornoway–
Ranish service until replaced
by Albion Viking BWG650B.
Thereafter, parked on the hill at
Cameron Terrace for its school
run, it could be guaranteed to start
in the morning, and if the Albion
Viking should fail to do so, it could
nip down to Ranish to take up the
first run. It also did the 9.15 p.m.
Saturday run from Stornoway in
case any of the passengers were the
worse for wear, but no church runs.
Withdrawn in August 1973, it was
looking the worse for wear when I
passed Loch's depot at Leurbost in
July 1974.

Bottom: What really surprised me
was coming across the cannibalised,
and probably vandalised, remains
of Dodge 3033PE by the roadside,
while driving up the A859 from
Tarbert to Stornoway in May 1989.
It had been common to chance
upon former buses and coaches in
all sorts of different guises, and in
varying degrees of disintegration,
all over the islands. When beyond
resale, it was often more economical
to sell them to islanders, who
were resourceful enough to give
them a new life as sheds, stores,
windshields, greenhouses, spare
rooms, mobile shops, bothies, etc.,
but not it seems 3033PE.

Top: An unusual heavyweight vehicle to run on Lewis was Leyland PS1/1 ORE641, operated by Galson-Stornoway Motor Services Limited of 1 Lower Barvas. They got it from Donald Mackay of Tain whose operation was acquired by Highland Omnibuses in October 1962, but without their vehicles. It was photographed at their garage at Tain with an unidentified withdrawn Leyland TD1 in the background, whose details have never appeared in any fleet list. (Robert Grieves Collection)

Middle: It was new to Berresford of Cheddleton with fleet number 18 in December 1947, with a thirty-five-seat dual-purpose Willowbrook body and a sliding front door, passing to Galson Motor Services in 1960. Parked at Stornoway, with a rebuilt destination box, it was regularly used on the service to Ness until withdrawn in December 1966, after which it was parked up at the depot at Lower Barvas and used as a store. (Robert Grieves Collection)

Bottom: Also parked at the depot at Lower Barvas were the vehicles that were not outstationed at drivers' houses, or up at Ness. The scene was captured on Saturday 16 September 1967, as KWY559 sits by the roadside behind ORE641, now withdrawn. The two little girls, I believe, lived in the house opposite, but it has not been possible to trace them to date.

Reregistered on entering civilian life, AST238C was a Bedford SB, new in 1952, with a Mulliner body. to the Royal Navy. It was acquired by Galson Motor Services from Malcolm McLennan of Govic in October 1966 as a twenty-nine-seat school bus, which had been used on his service from Husinish to Tarbert. It was kept at Brue for a school run from Barvas to Shawbost, and it also operated a church run from Shader to Barvas. Photographed in the evening of 7 May 1968 at the depot, it was about to be repainted, but would be withdrawn in May 1971.

Sinking in to the peats on Barvas moor is an Albion, still recognisable as a stalwart of John Mitchell's fleet: AV6600, acquired from Sutherland of Peterhead in 1948. An Albion Valkyrie, it was new in June 1934 to Kerr of Methlick as fleet number 9, with a locally built thirty-five-seat body by Walker of Aberdeen, and a rear entrance. In January 1944, it passed to Sutherland, as fleet number 27. Photographed in April 1968, it may have been a bothan rather than a bothy!

A Welcome from The Dean

Welcome to Worcester Cathedral. In the words and pictures of this guide you will glimpse people's efforts over the centuries to respond to God. For over a thousand years men, women and children have visited the building and used it in many ways and for many different purposes. The story of this place is really a story of its people, a story by no means finished.

This cathedral is a profoundly Christian place rooted in the person of Jesus and carrying his title and his mother's name. It remains an active centre of worship, prayer and care which, through its members, offers the hospitality of the generous loving God.

Gift yourself to be still in its space and time, and to know of its value to you.

Be refreshed and at peace, for God is with you.

This magnificent cathedral speaks to us equally of stability and of change. Although it has stood here for many centuries, it is important to remember that the great building we see today was by no means the first to be built on and around the site; also that it has undergone many changes and additions. Similarly its 'ownership' and prevailing patterns of worship have changed. So, to gain a proper understanding of the building we see now, we must look back over 1,500 years of history.

Apparently there were Christians in these parts as early as the Roman period, perhaps as early as the 4th century. Interesting evidence is provided by the discovery in 1970 of two graves, generally thought to be from Christian burials, beneath the undercroft of what is now called College Hall.

However it was not until the later 7th century that we have firm evidence of a Christian community existing here, when, in 680, the Diocese of Worcester was created and its first Bishop, Bosel, was installed. The first cathedral of the newly formed diocese, dedicated to St Peter, was no doubt a very primitive building.

It was in the days of King Edgar, the first monarch to unite the whole of England, that the saintly Oswald became Bishop in 961.

Oswald took the momentous step of founding a Benedictine monastic community at Worcester. In doing this, he provided the community with a new church, which was dedicated to St Mary. This was soon adopted as the cathedral church of the diocese in place of St Peter's, and may have been situated on the site of the nave of the present cathedral.

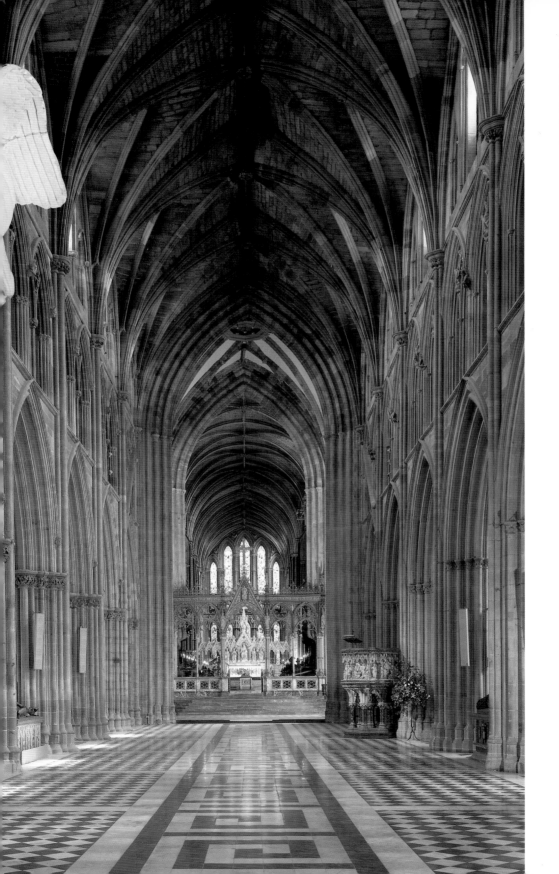

Recent excavations *side* the Chapter Hou*se* revealed a curving w*all* that may have been part of St Oswald's cathedral. ⑥

From AD961, for nearly 600 years, the cathedral was the centre of a thriving community of monks. They followed the Rule of St Benedict, in common with the monasteries in many parts of Europe. These religious houses kept alive not only the faith but also the tradition of classical learning during the dark ages which followed the collapse of the Roman Empire.

FAR LEFT: *The cloisters, the heart of the ancient monastery. Here monks worked, studied, taught and meditated.* ㉘

BELOW: *Norman arcading, probably incorporating reused Saxon pillar bases, above the stone seats where the monks received their visitors.* ㉕

The monks' central motto could be paraphrased thus: 'No work without prayer; no prayer without work.' These Benedictines ran what was a kind of welfare state inspired by Christian belief. They engaged in agriculture, education and works of scholarship. They entertained on a lavish scale, serving the needs of the thousands of pilgrims who thronged the precincts. They cared for the poor and needy, ran a hospital, gave sanctuary to criminals and managed their own estates. In the meantime, of course, the Mass was celebrated and the Offices, or corporate prayers, were recited or sung, day in day out, within the quire of the cathedral itself.

Things were on a small and simple scale in the days of Oswald, but Worcester began to gain in importance as a result of his canonization soon after he died in 992. His shrine became a place of pilgrimage. As time went on the number of monks grew from about 12 to 50. There came a setback when Worcester, like so many other monasteries across the land, fell victim to the Danish invader in 1041. Oswald's church was partially destroyed.

TOWER FACT FILE

- Built 1374, replacing one which fell down in 1175 and one taken down for safety in 1350.
- Height 52 metres (170 feet).
- Weight 4,500 tons.
- 235 steps to top.
- Clock 1869 by J.B. Joyce.
- 16 bells by John Taylor of Loughborough.
- Heaviest ringing bell 2500 kg (2.5 tons).

LEFT: *Embroidered panel of St Oswald by Leonard Evetts, a 20th-century Northumbrian artist and designer.* ⑨

From 1062 followed a period of creative growth under the leadership of the Saxon, Wulfstan. A monk and Prior of the monastery, he became Bishop of Worcester and, in due course, the second of Worcester's two great saints. Wulfstan's holiness and wisdom made him acceptable to the Norman invaders and his time as Bishop lasted longer than any of his contemporaries. He determined to rebuild the cathedral in the grand manner, even though he wept over the demolition of Oswald's simpler structure. Parts of his cathedral, built in the Romanesque (Norman) style, remain to this day. Most notable is the crypt, the largest Norman example in England, begun in 1084. With its remarkable forest of pillars this very ancient building still breathes an air of great mystery and devotion. It originally consisted of a central chapel, apsidal (semi-circular) at its east end, with three rows of eight stumpy columns. Steps down from the main church led to the two aisles, while around the east end ran an ambulatory, or processional path, where pilgrims could walk. At the eastern end

ABOVE: A 13th-century painting of an angel's face, from the Norman crypt, part of the original cathedral. ⑳

BELOW: The crypt. The symmetrical ranks of unadorned Norman columns breathe an atmosphere of great serenity. ⑳

LEFT: *The Norman doorway in the refectory building, leading from College Green through to the cloisters.* ③①

ABOVE: *Children admiring a model of how Bishop Wulfstan's church may have looked c.1120.* ②①

LEFT: *A bishop offering his church to God – a scene carved on a spandrel located in St Andrew's Chapel.* ⑭

were three chapels which were probably polygonal in shape.

Excavations show that the walls were once covered with painted and decorated plaster. Cracks indicate where the crypt was strengthened to prevent the Lady Chapel, begun a century and a half later, falling away from the rest of the building.

The completed crypt stretched back westwards as far as the present crossing. Traces of the Norman arches can still be seen in the present transepts. Because of the ravages of civil war and repeated fires, building and rebuilding continued all through the 12th century. This work is characterized by alternate bands of white and green stones. Of especial interest are the two western bays dating from the late 12th century and some very early work which show that the Norman cathedral extended west as far as the present building. The crypt was finished by 1089 when a great synod was held in it, and the monks moved into the new building.

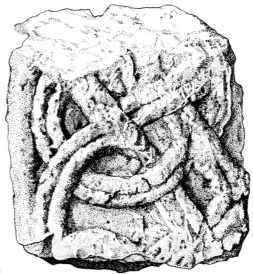

ABOVE: *A drawing of a 10th-century limestone fragment, once part of an altar screen, excavated in 1984 from beneath a column in the crypt.* ②⓪

As the church grew, so the surrounding monastery grew too, an almost continuous process of building and rebuilding. Most ancient of the monastic buildings is the early 12th-century Chapter House, prototype of several others such as those at Wells and Lincoln. Here monks transacted their daily business. Above the seats is a course of small circular arches inside larger intersecting ones. The windows and outer casing wall are 14th-century.

ABOVE: *The Worcester Antiphoner, c.1230, is a unique record of the musical worship of a medieval monastery.*

RIGHT: *The remains of the Guesten Hall, where visitors to the monastery stayed.*

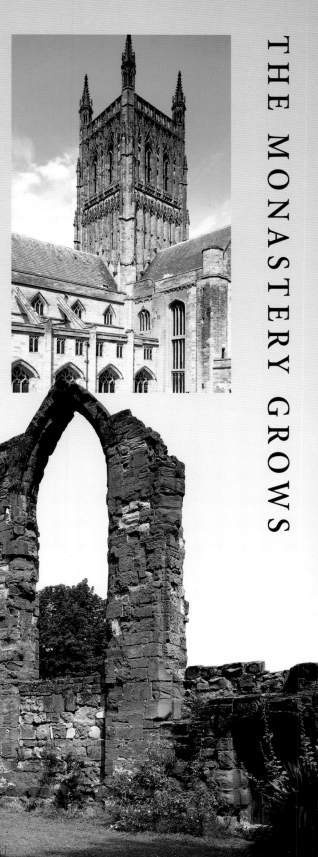

RIGHT: The tower, completed in 1374, represents the early Perpendicular style of architecture.

The cloisters were reconstructed at the end of the 14th century and beginning of the 15th. As well as linking the various parts of the monastery, they also served as a place where monks wrote and taught. Notable here is a series of carved bosses, especially the Jesse Tree in the south walk, beginning with Jesse himself (at the east end) and going through the kings of David's line to the Nativity of Christ.

The imposing refectory (or monk's dining room), on the south side of the cloisters, was rebuilt over a Norman undercroft. Now called College Hall, it has been used by the King's School since the Reformation. The 14th-century Guesten Hall where the monastery's guests were entertained was pulled down in 1862. Only its east wall survives as a ruin.

The precincts of the monastery were entered through the archway known as the Edgar Tower, probably also built in the 14th century. The monks' dormitory (beyond the west walk of the cloisters) and the infirmary (by the west end of the cathedral) now no longer exist. However, the visitor may gain a good impression of the monastic ensemble by viewing the scene from the far side of College Green.

THE MONASTERY GROWS

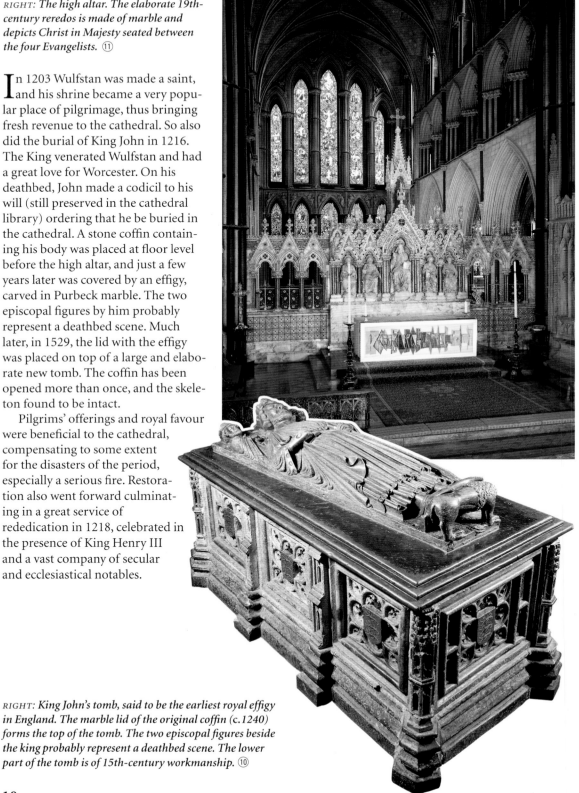

In 1203 Wulfstan was made a saint, and his shrine became a very popular place of pilgrimage, thus bringing fresh revenue to the cathedral. So also did the burial of King John in 1216. The King venerated Wulfstan and had a great love for Worcester. On his deathbed, John made a codicil to his will (still preserved in the cathedral library) ordering that he be buried in the cathedral. A stone coffin containing his body was placed at floor level before the high altar, and just a few years later was covered by an effigy, carved in Purbeck marble. The two episcopal figures by him probably represent a deathbed scene. Much later, in 1529, the lid with the effigy was placed on top of a large and elaborate new tomb. The coffin has been opened more than once, and the skeleton found to be intact.

Pilgrims' offerings and royal favour were beneficial to the cathedral, compensating to some extent for the disasters of the period, especially a serious fire. Restoration also went forward culminating in a great service of rededication in 1218, celebrated in the presence of King Henry III and a vast company of secular and ecclesiastical notables.

The quire, looking towards the nave and the west (Creation) window. In the foreground is King John's tomb; on the left, the bishop's seat, or cathedra. Beyond are the stalls where the monks said their Offices. The Office of Evensong is still sung here day by day.

ABOVE: *The Beauchamp tomb. Sir John Beauchamp, a favourite of Richard II, was treacherously beheaded for supposed treason. The monks of Worcester buried him in the cathedral.* ⑤

Not long after the rededication, Bishop William de Blois followed the fashion of the time by building a Lady Chapel behind the high altar. The bodies of many monks buried on the site were moved to a new charnel house near the north porch.

The Lady Chapel was built in the Early English style, with its characteristic sharply pointed arches, 'stiff leaf' foliage, and Purbeck marble columns. To it were added aisles and transepts, around which there ran a course of trefoil arches decorated with carved scenes, the most remarkable being the scenes of the Last Judgement in the south-east transept. So pleased was de Blois with his work that he decided to rebuild the quire in the same style. Throughout the 13th and 14th centuries the splendid Romanesque church of Wulfstan was progressively demolished and replaced by a cathedral in the new Gothic style of architecture.

The gifts of many pilgrims and continuing royal favour allowed rebuilding to continue beyond the quire and into the nave. The old church was steadily transformed, with the exception of the two western-most bays, which were allowed to stand.

Work halted in the middle of the 14th century at the two west bays on the north side. Building resumed some decades later on the south side but in a different architectural style, marking the transition from the Decorated to the Perpendicular which succeeded it.

The cause of the interruption was probably the Black Death, a bubonic plague which swept through Europe; the outbreak halved the population of Worcester. It may also have been that pilgrims were diverted away from Worcester to Gloucester where King Edward II was, most surprisingly, being venerated as a saint. The tourist trade was just as important in financial terms in those days as it is now!

Finally the great transept was re-formed and the tower completed as we see it today, while the central part of the nave was revaulted and the north porch added. By the end of the 14th century Worcester Cathedral as we know it was virtually complete.

BELOW: *The Nottingham alabaster, c. 1470, believed to have belonged to the Benedictine convent of White Ladies, Worcester. Traces of colour can still be seen.* ⑲

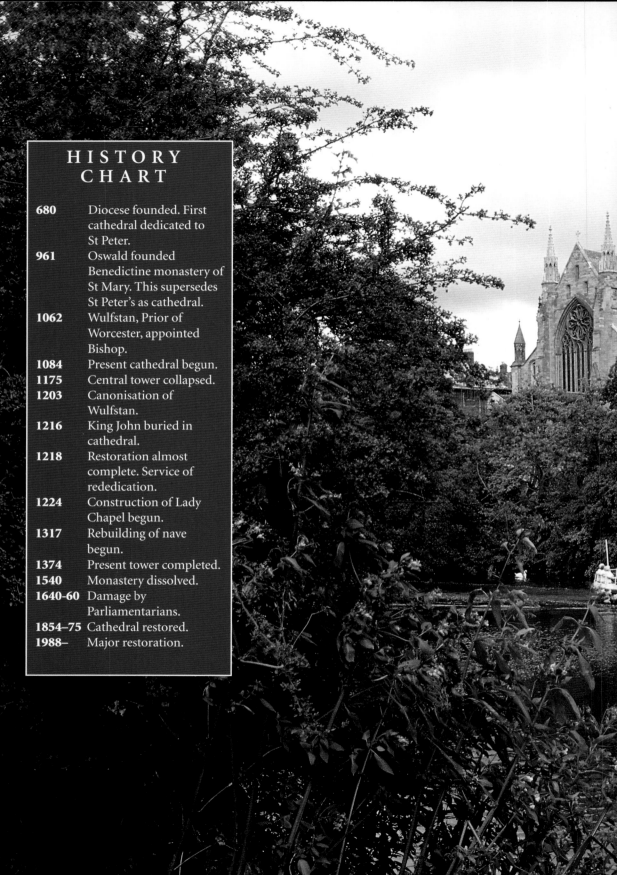

HISTORY CHART

680	Diocese founded. First cathedral dedicated to St Peter.
961	Oswald founded Benedictine monastery of St Mary. This supersedes St Peter's as cathedral.
1062	Wulfstan, Prior of Worcester, appointed Bishop.
1084	Present cathedral begun.
1175	Central tower collapsed.
1203	Canonisation of Wulfstan.
1216	King John buried in cathedral.
1218	Restoration almost complete. Service of rededication.
1224	Construction of Lady Chapel begun.
1317	Rebuilding of nave begun.
1374	Present tower completed.
1540	Monastery dissolved.
1640-60	Damage by Parliamentarians.
1854–75	Cathedral restored.
1988–	Major restoration.

Gande gaudet mater cu filio

LEFT: *A portrait in stained glass of Prince Arthur, elder brother of Henry VIII, who died at Ludlow in 1502 at the age of 16. This panel, from the south quire aisle, is an 18th-century copy of one in Malvern Priory completed around the time of Arthur's death. The strips of glass on each side are made up of stained and painted glass of many dates and styles, a reminder of what has been lost to the cathedral owing to the vandalism and changing tastes of bygone ages.*

BELOW AND TOP RIGHT: *Stonework, including the Tudor rose and pomegranate, adorns the south side of Prince Arthur's chantry.* ⑰

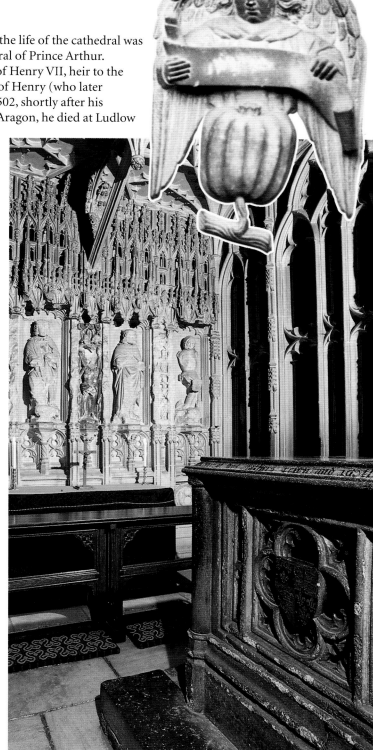

One great occasion in the life of the cathedral was the sumptuous funeral of Prince Arthur. Arthur was the elder son of Henry VII, heir to the throne and older brother of Henry (who later became Henry VIII). In 1502, shortly after his marriage to Catherine of Aragon, he died at Ludlow Castle at the age of 16. So, on Henry VII's death it was Arthur's brother who ascended the throne and who married Catherine. The funeral was followed by the erection of the great chantry which stands to the south of the high altar and contains Arthur's tomb. The outside wall of the chantry is covered with statues and imagery associated with the family. As one stands inside this chantry it is fascinating to reflect on how different the course of history might have been if the young Prince Arthur had survived and himself become king in place of his brother!

RIGHT: The interior of Prince Arthur's chantry. ⑰

The erection of Prince Arthur's chantry was the last major addition to the cathedral. The Reformation followed very shortly. The cathedral remained, but all else was changed. In 1540 the monastery was dissolved, after the shrines of Oswald and Wulfstan had been destroyed and their bodies reburied in an unknown place.

The cathedral was refounded with the constitution of a Dean and Chapter. The last Prior of the monastery, Henry Holbeach, became the first Dean. Under his successor, Dean Barlow, the screen across the nave was destroyed, the monks' stalls removed, and a large number of statues and windows destroyed or defaced.

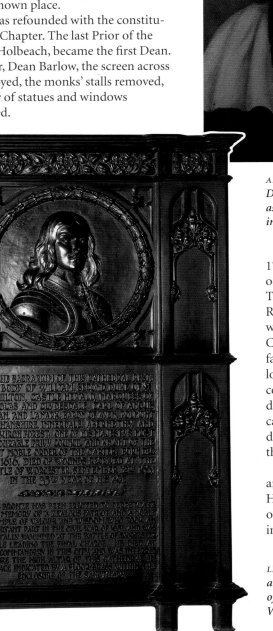

ABOVE: *One of Worcester's most learned of Deans, George Hickes. Appointed in 1683, as a non-juror Hickes was deprived of office in 1690.*

There was further damage in the 17th century, when Cromwell's troops occupied the nave and pillaged the city. The destruction continued during the Rebellion, except for the short period when Worcester was occupied by Charles II in 1651, culminating in the famous Battle of Worcester. The King lost the battle and fled. The Royalist commander, the Duke of Hamilton, died of wounds in the house near the cathedral known as the Commandery, and his body lies buried before the high altar.

With the restoration of the monarchy, and later the coming of the Hanoverians, there followed a period of calm, but the cathedral's fabric was in a parlous condition.

LEFT: *A plaque in the north quire aisle commemorating the 2nd Duke of Hamilton, killed at the Battle of Worcester (1651).* ⑫

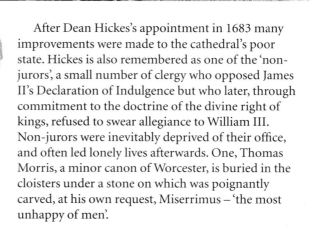

RIGHT: *The early 17th-century tomb in the south nave of clothier Robert Wilde and his wife Margaret. For 200 years his family lived at the Commandery.*

ORGAN FACT FILE

- 4 manuals and pedals.
- An amalgam of organs dating from 1842 (Hill; in the quire), 1874 (Hill; in the transept), 1894 (Hope Jones) further rebuilt by Nicholson (*c.*1908), Harrison (1925, 1967, 1972) and Wood Wordsworth (1978).
- 66 speaking stops and 4131 pipes ranging from 9.7 metres (32 feet) to 1 centimetre ($^1/_2$ inch).
- 2 electric-powered rotary blowers located in the crypt.

After Dean Hickes's appointment in 1683 many improvements were made to the cathedral's poor state. Hickes is also remembered as one of the 'nonjurors', a small number of clergy who opposed James II's Declaration of Indulgence but who later, through commitment to the doctrine of the divine right of kings, refused to swear allegiance to William III. Non-jurors were inevitably deprived of their office, and often led lonely lives afterwards. One, Thomas Morris, a minor canon of Worcester, is buried in the cloisters under a stone on which was poignantly carved, at his own request, Miserrimus – 'the most unhappy of men'.

LEFT: *Figures on the reredos of Prince Arthur's chantry, mutilated during Cromwell's Commonwealth.* ⑰

BELOW: *Detail of a monument in the north transept by Roubiliac to John Hough, Bishop 1717–43.*

During the 18th century many repairs and alterations of questionable quality took place. Much use was made of the whitewash brush. Tombs and monuments were moved all over the place.

The 19th century saw new life come into the Church as a whole. One of its effects at Worcester was a greater concern to preserve the fabric, and to make the cathedral a more glorious place for the worship of God. Hence the splendid Victorian restoration started in 1854, and carried through by such men as A.E. Perkins and Sir George Gilbert Scott. The present appearance of the cathedral is largely a result of this work.

Many windows were replaced, the most notable of the new ones being the very fine west window (1875) by J. Hardman Powell. By the removal of the organ and its screen from the entrance to the choir, an uninterrupted view from one end of the cathedral to the other was secured. Also belonging to this period are the west door, the nave pulpit, the choir screen, the bishop's throne, the reredos, the roof paintings and the magnificent paving which many think gives the cathedral a continental look.

Not all will approve of the very Victorian feel as a result of this restoration. It has however left us with one of the best collections of Victorian sculpture in England and some very fine stained glass. It is also clear that, if the restoration had not taken place, the cathedral would be but a ruin today.

RIGHT, ABOVE LEFT AND ABOVE RIGHT: **One of the most significant features of the Victorian restoration of Worcester Cathedral was the great west window, designed by J. Hardman Powell and installed in 1875. It depicts various aspects of the Creation story.** ①

BELOW: *The nave pulpit, installed during the Victorian restoration, is composed of several different marbles.* ⑥

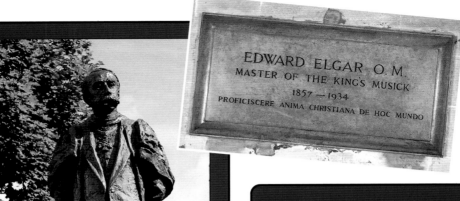

EDWARD ELGAR O.M.
MASTER OF THE KING'S MUSICK
1857 — 1934
PROFICISCERE ANIMA CHRISTIANA DE HOC MUNDO

EDWARD ELGAR

SIR EDWARD ELGAR

Worcester Cathedral was the emotional and visual backcloth to much of the life of the city's most famous son, composer Sir Edward Elgar (1857–1934). It was the 'concert hall' for performances of many of his works. Elgar is commemorated by the magnificent 'Gerontius' stained-glass window near the north door. It depicts scenes from his greatest choral master-piece, *The Dream of Gerontius*, which had its first successful British performance at Worcester Cathedral in 1902.

THE REV GEOFFREY STUDDERT KENNEDY

'Woodbine Willie', the greatest of the World War One padres, is commemorated by a plaque in the St George's Chapel. He was Vicar to Worcester's poorest parish from 1914 to 1922 and went to the battle-fronts of Europe as a chaplain to the troops, handing out New Testaments with one hand and packets of cigarettes with the other. He was awarded the Military Cross for bravery in rescuing wounded soldiers under heavy bombardment.

LEFT: The centre light of the 'Gerontius' window, erected to the memory of Sir Edward Elgar. The composer is also commemorated by the statue (far left), fittingly located where city and cathedral meet.

SIR CHARLES HASTINGS

Next to the 'Gerontius' window is another dedicated to the memory of Sir Charles Hastings, the remarkable 19th-century Worcester physician who founded the British Medical Association. He made the city a proud place of homage for the entire medical world in creating the BMA at a meeting in the board room of Worcester Royal Infirmary in 1832. The BMA now has many thousands of members in this country and overseas.

STANLEY BALDWIN

The ashes of Stanley Baldwin, three times Prime Minister of Britain, are buried in the nave near the west door. Baldwin, pictured below (left) with Sir Edward Elgar outside the cathedral, was noted for his great diplomacy in handling two of the biggest crises to hit the nation this century – the General Strike and the abdication of King Edward VIII. He led the Conservative Party from 1923 until his retirement from the Premiership in 1937.

Every 150 years or so, buildings of antiquity need major restoration. Worcester Cathedral is no exception and in 1988 a 20-year restoration programme was launched. The four piers holding up the tower have been strengthened. Large areas of stonework along the nave walls, the western face and western transepts have been renewed and their roofs repaired. After ten long years the scaffolding was dismantled and the distinctive view of the cathedral from the county cricket ground across the river can once more be seen, to the delight of journalists and cricket lovers alike. A new energy-efficient flood-lighting system to adorn the building by night has been generously donated.

In 1998, work commenced on the second phase of restoration – the quire, the eastern transepts and the Lady Chapel. After that will follow the 12th-century Chapter House and the cloisters, if there is any money left over! The cathedral has received substantial help from English Heritage, from the Cathedral Appeal Trust and from the many modern-day pilgrims and visitors. Most of the work has been done by the cathedral's own team of stone-masons, whose artistry is to be admired.

ABOVE AND BELOW: Two different skills being applied in the work to restore the cathedral. These skills are used not only to repair the fabric of the cathedral (below), but also to restore the decoration (above). Architects, archaeologists, carpenters, electricians, glaziers, plumbers and roofers also have important roles to play.

The cathedral's archaeologists have had a hand in the task too, recording every detail of the restoration for planning and posterity. Theirs is hidden but essential work.

One of the classic views of the English cricket scene.

BELOW: *The corner of the cathedral where candles are lit by visitors and pilgrims as the visible offerings of our innermost prayers.* ⑯

The stone walls enclose a sacred space. Everything the cathedral does is directed to the same end – the worship of God. This is the bishop's church and many services of the diocese of Worcester are held here, such as the ordination of priests, the commissioning of church workers, the gathering of young Anglicans and others for prayers and celebration. The city and the wider community come to mark important events. The judiciary come when the court is sitting; city councillors come when a new mayor is elected; health workers came to celebrate 50 years of the NHS. Hardly a week goes by without a major service of this kind, and all have to be meticulously planned by our liturgical team. The cathedral congregation of some 200 members are the core worshipping community through the year.

*ABOVE: **The bishop, surrounded by the Greater Chapter, licenses a new Dean.***

*ABOVE RIGHT: **The Worcester Festival Chorus rehearses for the Three Choirs Festival.***

*RIGHT: **Underneath are the everlasting arms.** This pietà by Glynn Williams, given by the Friends of the Cathedral and located in the crypt, epitomizes the sufferings of the 20th century.* ⑲

Worcester has always had a reputation for fine music, stimulated by the Three Choirs Festival which started here in 1717. The cathedral choir, while maintaining the great English choral tradition, has an ever-expanding repertoire which includes the best of 20th-century composition. Interest has been heightened thanks to the high profile given to choral music by popular radio stations such as Classic FM.

Worcester's choir can be heard singing in the cathedral on most days of the week; they also broadcast, tour and make records as well as going out to sing in the diocese. When they are not in residence, choirs visit from around the country and sometimes from overseas.

The cathedral receives hundreds of visitors each year from around the globe. Some of them come anonymously to find a quiet space for prayer and contemplation – the prayer candlestand in the Lady Chapel makes it one of the most used areas of the cathedral. Many schoolchildren come as part of their education. People are drawn as if by a magnet for a whole variety of experiences – historical, architectural, liturgical, archaeological, musical, artistic, educational and religious. The hospitality of God is for all to enjoy.

ABOVE LEFT: Rehearsals for one of a number of orchestral concerts held in the cathedral every year.

RIGHT: The cathedral at night.

BELOW AND ABOVE RIGHT: The cathedral choir in concert. Besides the demands of daily services, the choir has a busy programme of concerts and broadcasting.